Back in Control

The father of three children, GREGORY BODENHAMER worked as a juvenile probation officer for more than eight years and supervised some of southern California's worst-behaved children. Along with his associate Darlyne Pettinicchio, he created the Back in Control program to teach parents, teachers, school administrators, probation officers, social workers, and others how to control children's misbehavior.

Back in Control

How to Get Your Children to Behave

How to Get Your
Children to Behave

Gregory Bodenhamer

A FIRESIDE BOOK
Published by Simon & Schuster

FIRESIDE

Rockefeller Center
1230 Avenue of the Americas
New York, New York 10020

Published in 1988 by Prentice Hall Press
First Fireside Edition 1992

Originally published by Prentice-Hall, Inc.

FIRESIDE and colophon are trademarks of Simon & Schuster Inc.

Manufactured in the United States of America

29   30

Library of Congress Cataloging-in-Publication Data

Bodenhamer, Gregory.
Back in control.

Includes index.
1. Child rearing.   2.   Discipline of children.
I.   Title.
HQ769.B63845   1983   649'.64   82-24031
ISBN 0-671-76165-X

For my mother and father

Contents

Preface

This book is for "out-of-control" parents who want to regain control of their children's misbehavior. It was written with the assumption that your kids are already at least a couple of steps ahead of you—and increasing their lead. It is also assumed that you have tried any number of unsuccessful methods to get them to behave properly. You may have spanked them until your hand was red, reasoned with them until your throat was raw, "grounded" them until you felt more punished than they did. Or, finding little or no success in your methods, you may have applied the techniques described in other parenting books, or used the professional services of a psychiatrist, psychologist, marriage/family/ child therapist, or clinical social worker—without lasting results.

Fortunately, the concepts in this book should be significantly different from what you have read in magazines and other books or what you have been told by children's behavior experts.

Most of the popularly acclaimed parenting models used by experts encourage parents to use methods that were designed for mental health counseling. Mental health professionals assume that what works well for them will work just as well for parents. Unfortunately, that assumption is incorrect. Mental health counselors must rely on a number of different techniques and systems to motivate their patients to want to change. If patients enter therapy with the desire to make positive changes, great progress can be made. Many children, however, have no desire to change; they seem determined to have their way. Attempting to use counseling techniques to get better behavior from these kids is about as success-ful as using a counseling approach to get OPEC to lower oil prices.

As a result of their inability to get unmotivated children to change their ways, many mental health counselors began urging parents to be "democratic," to compromise or negotiate their rules away. And when that wasn't successful (when parents were still angry and resentful because of their children's behavior), they urged parents to allow children to have the "freedom to fail," to learn from the "natural consequences" of their misbehavior.

Children who are raised in "democratic" households, however, or in homes where there are few, if any, mandatory rules, sometimes have a difficult time adjusting to the firmer rules at school or on the job. They are frequently in trouble with their teachers or their bosses, and since they haven't been raised to obey other people's rules, they tend to blame others for their problems. The rules they do accept have, for the most part, come to them the hard way. They learn that fire is dangerous by being burned; or that stealing isn't worth the cost after they are repeatedly booked into Juvenile Hall; or, with ten or twenty years of reflection, that dropping out of high school was a stupid thing to do. After being allowed to fail at the important tasks of life—in the hope that they would learn from their failures—they have learned at least one thing: how to fail. Even worse, they see themselves as failures and act accordingly.

This is not meant to belittle the mental health profession. It does many things quite well. Changing the behavior of uncooperative kids, however, is not one of them. The greatest failure of the present state of affairs is that many children's counselors think parents don't have the ability, on their own, to change children's behavior.

Happily, they are wrong. Most childhood misbehavior, as you will see, is not the direct result of inherited rottenness; diseases of the mind or body; social or economic woes; television, movies, and rock music; or other situations beyond parental control. A child's misbehavior is simply an exercise of power—doing what he or she wants to do in the absence of active parental authority.

By focusing on the use of power within the family, and by applying a simple three-step formula, you will learn to control virtually any type of children's misbehavior without hiring an expert to "fix" the kids; without punishment, compromises, and bargains; and without throwing the kids out the front door.

By using your parental authority to take control of your children's problem behavior, you will not only develop well-behaved, self-disciplined children, you will also end the distress that accompanies misbehavior. And best of all, you will get to share a more fulfilling love—for well-behaved children are much easier to love and appreciate than those who constantly flout your rules.

Your children will also benefit from your exercise of parental authority. Inasmuch as they will be obeying the rules you set down for them, they will no longer be confronted by the anger, rage, resentment, or rejection that springs from your frustration at not getting them to behave properly. And when you use Back in Control, you will find that your children will obey, accept, and eventually embrace the behavioral rules you believe to be vital for their well-being. They will grow up believing that they can succeed in doing what is required of them. Failure of achievement—in controlling their behavior—will not be a part of their childhood experience. Nor, if you are willing to devote time and energy to the Back in Control program, will failure of achievement be a part of your parenting experience.

Above all others, you as a parent can get your children to behave properly. Even if the situation appears to be hopeless, parents are almost always able to regain control in their homes. The exceptions usually involve parental incapabilities due to alcohol or drug abuse, severe emotional disorders, or a lack of love for the child.

My associates and I have successfully shown thousands of parents how to control their children's misbehavior. In our Back in Control workshops for parents we typically show parents how to stop alcohol and drug abuse, truancy, procrastination, arguments, running away, temper tantrums, and school failure. In the Parents in Control program that we created and operate for the Orange County, California, Probation Department, we have shown parents of some of southern California's most delinquent, criminally oriented kids how to stop their children from robbing, burglarizing, vandalizing, dope dealing, and assaulting.

We have worked with families whose children are as young as three and as old as twenty. Our families have wanted help with everything from keeping a four-year-old in bed at night to stopping a seventeen-year-old heroin addict from using and "dealing." We have helped parents keep chronic bed-wetters dry (one was twenty years old) and "poopers" (children who foul their clothing while awake) clean and fresh. We have even shown moms who have been repeatedly beaten by their children how to regain control. And if they can do it, so can you—if you are willing to be powerful. Power, however, belongs to those who use it; and if *you* don't, *your kids* will.

All situations in this book are true. Names and identifying characteristics have been changed to protect the privacy of parents and children.

ACKNOWLEDGMENTS

To Randall M. Foster, M.D., and Paul Wood, M.D., who believe in the power of parents and of clearly stated rules.

To Darlyne Pettinicchio, who is not only my partner, but also the best probation officer I have ever known.

To Emma Failla, my dependable, cheerful, and enthusiastic typist.

To my wife, Terrie, who combines encouragement and enthusiasm with appropriate doses of humility.

And to the thousands of families with whom we have worked: Without them this book could not exist.

Back in Control

1

Arthur, Ken, and Emma

ARTHUR—THE CHORE HATER

Jean, forty-five and divorced, should have been in good spirits. They'd had the closing on the house she just sold; there was money in the bank—she would be able to pay her bills up to date for the first time in weeks; and her seventeen-year-old daughter, Melinda, had just been awarded a scholarship from the University of California. But Jean was tense, irritable, and on the verge of anger—and, as it turned out, with justification. As she suspected, her fourteen-year-old-son, Arthur, hadn't done any of his daily chores. The dishes were still in the sink from last night, his room was a mess, the living room floor that he was supposed to have vacuumed was covered with litter and food droppings, and Arthur, ignoring it all, was watching television and eating cookies.

Jean restrained herself with great effort and attempted to use what she had read in several parenting books:

"Arthur, it makes me very angry when you don't follow through and do the things you've agreed to do. Last week you complained about all the yard work you had to do and said if Melinda would trade housework with you, you would do the dishes everyday and the floor at least three times a week. So far you haven't done anything."

Arthur looked up at his mom, said, "As soon as this program is over, I'll get busy," and went back to watching reruns of "Happy Days."

Jean, not wanting to be unreasonable, let Arthur finish out "Happy Days" while she went to change her clothes. Twenty minutes later she

1

returned to find Arthur watching "LaVerne and Shirley." The floor had not been vacuumed, no dishes had been done, and his room was still a mess. Her resolve to be reasonable and trusting was overcome by a wave of anger and resentment.

"Dammit, I can't count on you to do anything. You won't even follow through with your own agreements. You can see what a filthy mess this house is but you aren't willing to do a thing. Your sister and I have to do everything. I work hard day after day to do my share around here, and Melinda more than does her part. And what do you do? *Nothing!* Nothing but watch television."

Arthur stood up and threw his bag of cookies on the floor. "Living with you is like living in a prison. You think you're a damn warden. Everything has to be your way, when you want it. You don't care about me or what I want."

"If you don't like it here, you can get out any time you please."

Arthur, taking his mother at her word, left the house in a huff and spent the evening at a friend's house watching television. His mother and Melinda worked in angry silence vacuuming the floor and doing the dishes. The next morning, Jean enrolled her family in a Back In Control workshop.

KEN—THE DOPE DEALER

Ken liked dope. He liked to smoke it, he liked to snort it, and he really liked the money he earned from selling it. The kids at his high school knew him as a dealer you could always "score" from. His room was like a small showroom for drugs. He had posters on the wall glorifying its use, several pieces of jewelry made to look like marijuana leaves, and the tools of the trade—scales, manicuring equipment, baggies, cigarette rolling papers, and a drawerful of cash for easy transactions.

He was almost seventeen years old and had been dealing dope for three years. If his parents hadn't dried out in an alcohol treatment program, Ken would probably have continued dealing into adulthood. But once free of alcohol, his parents saw what their son was doing and brought Ken to a Back In Control workshop.

EMMA—THE TRUANT

Betty walked into Emma's room to wake her up. It was already after 6:30 and Emma would have to hurry if she was going to get to school on time today.

"Emma, get up. Emma, it's time to get up," said Betty, gently tugging at her daughter's shoulder.

"All right, all right!" said Emma, pushing her mom's arm away. "I'll get up. Just leave me alone!" and turned back over.

Betty returned to her room to finish dressing so she could get to work on time. She looked in on Emma about fifteen minutes later and found her asleep again.

"Emma, Emma, it's time to get up," she said sharply.

"Leave me alone!" snapped Emma.

"You're going to be late for school."

"No I won't, just leave me alone and I'll get up on my own."

"But you don't. You've missed two days of school already this week." And Betty reached down to pull Emma out of bed.

"Don't touch me, bitch!"

"Don't talk to me that way, dammit!" she screamed. "I'm your mother and I'm going to get more respect than that!" And she slapped Emma across the face.

But Emma returned the blow with even greater force and doubled up her fist ready to defend herself. Betty, not knowing what to do next and not wanting to have a fist fight with her daughter, ran from the room and went to work. Emma missed that entire day of school, her third in a row and the tenth that month.

After she got to work that morning, Betty called our office on the advice of Emma's school counselor and enrolled in a Back In Control workshop.

We will rejoin Arthur, Ken, Emma, and their parents at the conclusion of this book.

2

Mandatory, Optional, and Discretionary Rules

MANDATORY RULES

A mandatory rule is one that children *must* obey. Parents clearly state the rule, effectively follow through to make sure it is obeyed, and enforce it consistently.

Your children weren't delivered from the womb with knowledge of your rules, the desire to obey them, or even an understanding that you expect your rules to be obeyed. For the first few years of their lives, you literally made your children abide by your rules: You effectively followed through and consistently controlled what they ate, where they pooped and peed (in diapers for the first couple of years), what they wore, where they went, and for the most part, what they did. When they started walking, you began giving clearly stated rules—"No," "Don't," "Stop"— in addition to consistently and effectively following through to see that your rules were obeyed. And you were wonderfully successful at getting your children to obey those rules. To see just how successful you were, please indicate on the following pages how you got your children to bathe regularly, use acceptable table manners, and generally behave better in other people's homes than in their own.

Most children bathe regularly by family standards. Do your children bathe regularly, or do you have to hose them down in their sleep?

Assuming you have been successful, how did you get your children to bathe regularly? (Choose the primary method):

5

1. When they were infants, I consistently bathed them myself. And when they were old enough to get in the bathub on their own, I told them, when necessary, to take a bath whether they wanted to or not, and I effectively followed through to see that they did.
2. I prayed a lot.
3. I took them to an expert.
4. I gave them the "freedom to fail." When they became so dirty and ill that they couldn't stand it, they bathed.
5. I reasoned with them.
6. I didn't.do anything. They were born knowing the importance of bathing.
7. I bargained, negotiated, or compromised with them.
8. I rewarded or punished them.
9. I was tough! I told them to bathe regularly or get out of the house.

Most children, on the basis of their age and abilities, use table manners acceptable to their parents. Do your children generally use acceptable table manners or do waiters and waitresses smirk, laugh, or point at your children in disgust?

Assuming you have been successful, how did you get your children to use proper table manners? (Choose the primary method):

1. From the time they were old enough to sit at a kitchen or dining-room table, whenever I saw them using bad manners, I consistently told them to eat properly whether they wanted to or not, and effectively followed through to see that they did.
2. I prayed a lot.
3. I took them to an expert.
4. I gave them the "freedom to fail." After repeatedly making fools of themselves in front of friends and relatives, they decided to start using decent table manners.
5. I reasoned with them.
6. I didn't do anything. They were born holding a copy of Emily Post's book of etiquette.
7. I bargained, negotiated, or compromised with them.
8. I rewarded or punished them.
9. I was tough! I told them to eat properly or get out of the house.

Most children, by their parent's standards, behave better in other people's homes than in their own. Do your children behave better in other people's homes, or does your host or hostess have to keep getting on them about their misbehavior?

Assuming you have been successful, how did you get your children to behave better in the homes of your friends and relatives than in your own homes? (Choose the primary method):

1. From the time they could walk, I consistently told them to behave well, and effectively followed through to see that they did. In general, I kept tighter control over their behavior when we were visiting than when we were at home.
2. I prayed a lot.
3. I took them to an expert.
4. I gave them the "freedom to fail." After all of our friends and relatives stopped asking us over, they decided to start behaving better.
5. I reasoned with them.
6. I didn't do anything. They were born knowing the importance of being a good guest.
7. I bargained, negotiated, or compromised with them.
8. I rewarded or punished them.
9. I was tough! I told them to behave politely or leave home.

If you were successful at getting your children to obey any or all of those typical mandatories, you can see that you did the following:

Clearly stated your rules
Effectively followed through to demonstrate that the rules must be obeyed
Were consistent

But, as children become older and more capable of rational reasoning, many parents adjust their parenting styles to fit the maturing child. They either adopt popularly acclaimed "new" approaches, or they begin to take their early successes for granted and, often unknowingly, allow their mandatory rules to become optional.

OPTIONAL RULES

An optional rule is one that parents want obeyed, but that children find ways to evade. Either the rule hasn't been clearly stated, or the parents haven't effectively followed through to make sure that it is obeyed, or the parents haven't been consistent in applying the rule, or all three. Most parenting theories and programs are either consciously designed to give children options, or are flawed in their design to the point where children make their own options.

If you have spent months or years unsuccessfully trying to change your children's behavior, answer the following questions to see why you aren't in control.

Rewards and Punishments. If your primary method of getting your children to obey your rules is rewards or punishments—and they are willing to put up with your punishments and forego your rewards—who's in control, you or the kids?

Problem Solving (Bargaining, Negotiating, Compromising). If your primary method of getting your children to obey your rules is bargaining, negotiating, or compromising—and your children are good negotiators or don't live up to their agreements—who's in control, you or the kids?

Freedom to Fail. If your primary method of getting your children to obey your rules is allowing them the "freedom to fail"—and they don't learn the lesson you hoped they would—who's in control, you or the kids?

Reasoning. If your primary method of getting your children to obey your rules is reasoning—and your children don't agree with your reasoning—who's in control, you or the kids?

Experts. If your primary method of getting your children to obey your rules is reliance on an expert—and the expert isn't able to motivate your children to change—who's in control, you or the kids?

Inherited Insight. If your primary method of getting your children to obey your rules is reliance on the knowledge they brought with them from the womb—and their instincts don't agree with your rules—who's in control, you or the kids?

Praying. If your primary method of getting your children to obey your rules is prayer—and God doesn't choose to make your children obey your rules—who's in control, you or the kids?

Getting Tough. If your primary method of getting your children to obey your rules is telling them to obey or leave the house—and they are willing to leave your house instead of obeying your rules—who's in control, you or the kids?

The answer to these questions should be self-evident. Children will not go out of their way to obey rules they don't believe in, and if you provide options for them to do things their way, sometimes they will take advantage.

If you don't clearly state your rules, whose interpretation of those rules are your children likely to use, yours or theirs?

If you don't effectively follow through and enforce your own rules, are your children likely to follow through and enforce them on themselves? Are your children likely to be consistent in obeying rules that you aren't consistent in enforcing?

Children obey mandatory rules not because they necessarily want to, but because they have no choice. The rules are stated clearly to avoid, or at least to minimize, misinterpretation and misunderstanding. Parents not only follow through to see that the rule is obeyed, but to the best of their ability make sure that it is *consistently* obeyed.

Children, however, like the rest of us, prefer doing what they want, when they want. And if parents provide an opportunity, kids will sometimes take advantage and turn parents' mandatory rules into "optionals."

DISCRETIONARY RULES

A discretionary rule is one that children have parental permission to set for themselves.

There is nothing wrong with discretionary rules. Depending on age, maturity, and experience, children should be able to exercise their discretion in many things. Furthermore, discretionary rules are *always* better than "optionals." Rules should either be mandatory—parent's choice—or discretionary—children's choice. Anything in between causes anger, resentment, and frustration.

3

Why Are They So Rotten?

Children aren't born wanting to obey—or disobey—the rules set down by parents, schools, or society. And one of the great stumbling blocks in getting children to behave "properly" is the human desire to do as one pleases. In fact, that desire is such an essential, but so often overlooked, element of human behavior that I am promulgating it as "Bodenhamer's Law" to focus attention on it.

BODENHAMER'S LAW

> Human beings (including children) prefer doing things in their own way, in their own time, and given an option, will sometimes do as they please.

Keeping this basic "law" of human behavior in mind, the reasons children misbehave aren't nearly as complicated or complex as you may believe. There are almost always rational, logical, and clearly understandable reasons for children's misbehavior. Children frequently have what they consider very good reasons for doing as they please, and if you will answer the following questions as the child in each situation would, you will begin to see why they don't obey your rules.

You are a ten-year-old girl who enjoys watching television after dinner, but you are supposed to do the dishes as soon as dinner is over. What would you prefer:

A. Getting up and doing the dishes even though you will miss a good program?
B. Your mother leaving you alone to watch television?

You are a sixteen-year-old boy who likes the excitement, comradeship, and effect of smoking dope. Your parents are always on your back about dope smoking and your "scummy" friends. What would you prefer:

A. Staying home with your parents, dope free?
B. Smoking some dope with your friends?

You are a fifteen-year-old boy with homework in English, your worst subject. You are watching an R-rated movie with a lot of nudity on Home Box Office. What would you prefer:

A. Doing your homework?
B. Continuing to watch the movie?

You are a sixteen-year-old girl. Your very special boyfriend has driven you to a secluded park. He holds you close and tells you he loves you very much. You are flushed with excitement and anticipation as he touches an intimate part of your body. What would you prefer:

A. Telling him you are not that type of girl and demanding that he take you home?
B. Practicing to make grandparents out of your parents?

You are a fourteen-year-old boy. You hate school and are behind in all of your subjects. Your teachers make disparaging remarks about your lack of effort. You have recently made two new friends who often cut school to play computer games at a nearby arcade. They are encouraging you to do the same. What would you prefer:

A. Staying at school in class while your friends are having fun?
B. Cutting school and going to the arcade with your friends?

You are an eleven-year-old girl. Your parents are constantly bugging you to do chores. As soon as you finish with one you have to start another. Not only do the chores seem to be never-ending, but also your parents never seem to be satisfied and are always yelling at you. What would you prefer:

A. Pleasing them by speeding up and doing the tasks as fast as you can?
B. Taking control of the situation and making their day unpleasant, too, by taking as long as possible to do your chores?

As a parent, your long experience with your children should tell you that if they are given an option, they will sometimes take advantage of it and do as they please. In the foregoing examples, the children don't necessarily want to be defiant or disobedient. They are simply young human beings who prefer doing things in their own way, in their own time, just like the rest of us. And unless parents make a mandatory rule against such behavior, the kids will probably do as they please.

4

How You Got Out of Control: Unclear Directions

> Human beings (including children) prefer doing things in their own way, in their own time, and given an option, will sometimes do as they please.

If you don't clearly state your rules, whose interpretation of those rules are your children likely to use, yours or theirs?

From your experience as a parent, you should know that your kids will use your words to their advantage. If you don't clearly state your rule, it doesn't matter how consistently you follow through and enforce it, for you don't have a "mandatory." Instead, you have an inexact, indistinct, vague, and ill-defined rule that your children will use to their advantage.

To establish a mandatory rule, you must deal exclusively with behavior and tell the child specifically what to do or not to do, including, if appropriate, the how, when, and where of it. Clearly stated rules do not include questions, requests, expectations, advice, predictions, observations, threats, sarcastic encouragement, rewards, challenges, or an excess of words. And perhaps most importantly, they do not deal with the child as the problem.

TRYING TO CHANGE THE CHILD

Darlyne was furious. Her sixteen-year-old son had come home under the influence of alcohol for the third time in two weeks. He wasn't drunk, but his eyes were red, his speech a little slurred, and he smelled like the crowd at a Willie Nelson concert.

"It's after one o'clock in the morning! Where in the hell do you get off causing me so much worry! I saw your dad through ten years of nights like this and I couldn't stand it. Now you're trying to be just like him. I can't count on you any more than I could on him. You're undependable! You're worthless! You don't give a damn about anybody but yourself."

Tim started toward his bedroom, but Darlyne, frustrated, and fearful that her words were true, chased him with more angry words. "Don't turn your back on me, you little drunk. You're going to hear everything I have to say."

"I have heard it Mom!" said Tim, now angry at his mother and her hurting words. "I heard it when you said it to dad, and I've heard it almost every day since dad left. Leave me alone!" and he rushed out the door to spend the night on the street.

At no point did Darlyne tell Tim, "Don't drink alcohol," or "Don't come home late." She obviously felt frustrated, angry, and helpless. And Tim, hearing her angry words, became angry himself. But rather than put up with them for yet another time, he stormed out of the house, physically and emotionally away from his mother. Darlyne treated Tim, rather than his behavior, as the problem. No mandatory rule was set.

GUILT

Eleven-year-old George would rather watch television than do dishes, would rather watch television than do homework, would rather watch television than do yardwork. And his experience told him that most of the time he could do just that—watch television instead of doing anything else.

One Saturday morning during the middle of "The Bugs Bunny-Roadrunner Show," George failed to get up and clean his bedroom as his mother told him to do for the fifth time. Instead, he screamed at her to leave him alone. Out of frustration and anger, she ran crying from the room. Dad, doing his duty, came in to talk to George and walked between his son and the television set.

"Don't you know what you're doing to your mom? You're tearing her up inside. All she wants you to do is cooperate. She doesn't ask much of you, she doesn't require much of you, only that you pull your own weight around here."

George tilted in his seat so he could see Wiley Coyote mashed under a boulder.

"Don't you even have the courtesy to look me in the face when I'm talking to you?" asked his father. "You don't seem to care about me, your mother, or anyone else in this family."

George rolled his eyes and cast a deep sigh, looked his father square in the face, and "tuned him out." Dad, in disgust, threw his hands in the air and walked away saying, "I give up! I don't know what's wrong with you, but it's obvious that you don't care about anybody but yourself."

George's father, with the best of intentions, is trying to motivate his son to change his behavior through guilt. However, he didn't tell George specifically to do or not to do anything. No mandatory rule was set.

THE BROKEN CHILD

Sally is fourteen. She doesn't like to do chores or homework, come home on time, or go to school regularly, and she hangs out with a group of kids who smoke dope. Her parents have done almost everything to get her to "straighten up."

Sally was getting ready to go to school when her mother and father came in and sat on her bed. "Honey," said mom, "we've tried everything to help you. We've tried to reason with you, we've been to parenting programs, we took you to the psychiatrist, and nothing seems to work. We don't know why you're the way you are, but we do want you to know that we love you and that we'll do everything we can for you."

Sally looked at her dad, then at her mom, with a cynical glare and said, "All right, I hear it coming. What do you have planned now?"

"We've decided after talking to your psychiatrist that the best thing for you is the adolescent treatment unit at Shady Acres Hospital."

Instead of concentrating on Sally's behavior, her parents decided to have her "fixed." As long as parents see the problem as the child rather than the child's behavior, it is unlikely that they will successfully change the behavior.

Some children benefit from treatment programs in psychiatric hospitals. But others are placed there because of behavior problems when parents have not consistently stated and enforced their rules. And if nothing changes at home, it is unlikely that any lasting behavior change will result.

CLICHÉS AND WORN-OUT
EXPRESSIONS

If you tell your children, "shape up," "try harder," "get that chip off your shoulder," "get your act together," "your attitude stinks," "ease up"—what, specifically, are they to do or not do?

From your experience, if you use these or similar expressions, do your children do what you want them to do, or do they tend to argue and show resentment?

UNSPECIFIC DIRECTIONS

If you say, "Be home on time," to your children, whose definition of "on time" are they likely to use, yours or theirs?

If you say, "Be nice to your sister," who gets to determine what "being nice" means, you or the kids?

If you say, "Don't drink too much," who gets to determine what "too much" means, you or the kids?

Or if you say, as one set of parents did, "Don't smoke bad dope," who gets to determine what "bad dope" is, you or the kids?

From your experience, if you aren't specific, are your children likely to go out of their way to figure out what you really want them to do?

REQUESTS AND FAVORS

If you say, "Please pick up your clothes now," are your children likely to believe that they must pick up the clothes now, or that you are merely making a polite request?

If you say, "I would appreciate it if you would be home at nine tonight," are your children likely to believe that they must be home at nine tonight, or that you would merely show appreciation if they came home at nine tonight?

If you say, "If you wouldn't mind, I'd like the lawn mowed," are your children likely to think that they must mow the lawn, or that you merely would like them to mow it?

If you say, "Will you do me a favor and not smoke dope anymore," are your children likely to believe that they must stop smoking dope, or merely that you want another favor?

From your experience, if you merely request that your children change their problem behavior, are they likely to honor your request?

ADVICE

If you tell your children, "You drink too much," do they hear that they must stop or cut down on their drinking, or merely that you think they drink too much?

If you say, "If I were you, I'd study more," do your children hear that they must study more, or only that you think they should study more?

If you say, "Why do I have to keep telling you that smoking is bad for you," do your children hear that they must quit smoking, or that you are compelled to keep telling them that smoking is bad?

From your experience, are your children likely to change their "problem" behavior on the basis of your advice?

PREDICTIONS

If you say, "If you don't quit cutting school, you'll never graduate from high school and you'll never get a decent job," do your children hear that they must stop cutting school, or that you think they'll turn into bums if they don't?

If you say, "You'll wind up in prison," after they're caught stealing for the third time, do they hear that they must not steal, or that you believe that they're going to wind up in prison?

If you say, "You're going to be a drunk just like your father," do they hear a rule against drinking or a prediction that they're going to be a drunk just like their father?

If you say, "You're never going to get off restriction," after they come home late again, do your children hear that they must come home on time, or that you believe they're going to be on restriction for a long time?

From your experience, do predictions of unpleasant or dire consequences consistently motivate your children to change their behavior?

WANTS, DESIRES,
AND EXPECTATIONS

If you say, "I want you to pick up your clothes off the bedroom floor now," do your children hear that they must pick their clothes up, or only that you want them to?

If you say, "I'd like you to help me in the yard today," do the children hear that they must help you in the yard today, or that you'd merely like their help?

If you say, "I expect you to quit hitting your sister," does she hear that she must stop hitting her sister or only that you expect her to?

From your experience, are your wants, desires, and expectations sufficient to get your children to obey your rules?

THREATS, REWARDS,
AND CONSEQUENCES

If you say, "Just wait until your father gets home, he'll make you clean your room," does the child have to clean his room, or merely have to wait until father gets home?

If you say, "If you come home late one more time, you're grounded for a week," do the children have to come home on time, or merely have to be willing to take the consequences of staying out late?

If you say, "You may go out tonight if you finish your book report," does the child have to finish the book report, or merely have to be willing to give up the reward?

From your experience, have you successfully and consistently changed your children's problem behavior with threats, rewards, or consequences?

PLEADING AND BEGGING

If you say, "Won't you even talk to me nicely," do the children hear a rule to speak to you in a specific fashion, or a pleading request to speak "nicely"?

Based on your words, if you say, "Please, just once, don't come home drunk," does the child hear a demand that he not drink, or the pleadings of a helpless parent?

If the parent says, "My God, I'm only asking for a little coopera-tion. You can see that the floor is a mess," does the child hear a rule telling her to vacuum the floor right away, or a pleading for cooperation?

From your experience, can parents successfully change a child's problem behavior through begging or pleading?

SARCASTIC ENCOURAGEMENT

If a parent says, "Here, let me help you pack," when the child complains about household rules, does the child hear a specific rule against leaving home, or does he hear that he may leave at his own discretion?

If a parent says, "You know it all! Go ahead and try it!" does the child have a clear direction that he is not to smoke dope, or encourage-ment to learn the lesson the hard way?

If a parent says, "Do it, if you think you're man enough," to a child who is mad enough to hit him, does the child have a direct demand that he not hit the parent, or encouragement to go ahead and "duke it out"?

From your experience, is sarcastic encouragement to misbehave effective at changing children's problem behavior?

OBSERVATIONS AND OPINIONS

If a parent says, "Your room is a mess and you need to do something about it," is the parent directing the child to clean the room, or merely making an observation as to its untidy state and what the child needs to do?

If a parent says," "You're late again," is the child being given a clear direction as to when she is to be home, or is the parent merely making an observation?

If a parent says, "This report card is horrible," is the child being told to do well in school, or is the parent merely giving an opinion?

From your experience, are parental observations effective in chang-ing children's problem behavior?

QUESTIONS

If a parent asks, "Where were you?" is the child being told to come home on time or to be at a certain place, or is the parent merely asking a question?

If the parent asks, "Why did you steal that tire?" is the child being told not to steal, or does he merely have to answer the parent's question?

If a parent asks, "What made you think you could get away with smoking dope on campus?" does the child hear a direct demand that she not smoke dope, or a question?

From your experience, is questioning a child's misbehavior an effective way to change it?

REASONS

If a parent says, "I've talked to you until I'm blue in the face about the importance of school. You know if you don't do well in junior high, you'll never do well in high school; and if you don't do well in high school, you won't be able to get into a good college; and if you don't get into a good college, you won't be able to get the best opportunities available to you. Your whole life is going to be ruined unless you start making some changes. You have homework every night; I've talked to your teachers. You know how important it is that you keep up with your work, or at least you *should* know. I've told you enough. And you have homework tonight. Are you doing it? No! You're watching television. Night after night of television. What is television ever going to get you? It won't get you a good job. It won't get you into a good college. All it does is eat up precious time that you could be using for studying," does the child hear a rule that he do homework, or does he hear so many words that he simply tunes the parent out?

From your experience, are your children likely to change their problem behavior if you dump a ton of words in their ears?

CHALLENGES

If a father angrily states, "You will be home at seven tonight," does the child hear a rule relating to his behavior, a prediction of where he will be at seven tonight, or a challenge?

If a mother angrily states, "You aren't going to leave this house," is the child hearing a direct demand telling her to stay in the house, a prediction of what will happen in the future, or a challenge?

From your experience, can you count on children to obey angry challenges?

CONFLICTING DIRECTIONS/RULES

If dad says, "Be home at six tonight for dinner," and mom says, "No, there's no need for him to be home before seven," and the parents argue about what time the child should be home, does the child know that he must be home at a certain time, or does he think he may choose his own time?

If a child hears her mother say, "No, you may not have another cookie. We're going home soon," yet grandma says, "Now, don't be silly, little girls need all the cookies they can eat," does the child have a clear rule that she not eat the cookie, or permission to eat to her heart's content as long as she eats at grandma's house?

If a teacher calls dad and says, "Jamie isn't doing his homework. I wonder if you could help him get it done?" and dad says to Jamie, "That damn teacher called again. I want you to get him off my back," does Jamie hear that he must do his homework, or that as far as Dad is concerned, the teacher is the problem?

From your experience, do children respond well to conflicting rules?

TIMELESS DIRECTIONS

If mom says, "Take out the trash," but doesn't say when it's to be taken out, is the child likely to take it out "now," or choose his own time, instead?

If dad says, "Don't smoke dope," does the child hear a demand that she "never" smoke dope, or might she interpret it to mean she is merely not to smoke dope "now," or until dad cools off?

If mom says, "Sit up straight," and the child sits up each time she says it, does he hear that he must never slouch in a chair, or that the only time he has to sit up straight is when mom tells him to?

From your experience, if parents don't tell children when and how often a rule is to be obeyed, are the kids likely to use their parent's time standards or their own?

GUIDELINES FOR CLEAR
DIRECTIONS

In general, when attempting to regain control of your children's misbehavior, use a firm and resolute voice that sounds as though you mean what you say, and tell them *what to do, when to do it, and how often it is to be done.*

Begin your directions with words describing an element of time (now, never, always) or a verb (stop, quit, start, don't, be, take, make, mow, do). Add when and how often you want the rule obeyed. The fewer words you use, the better. Extra words cause blank stares, angry confrontations, misunderstood directions, and a host of other problems. If your children are already pretty good about obeying a particular rule, you may start with "please" or other polite terms as long as the children continue to obey the rule.

Start using those directions that most clearly state your rule. If your children's standards of cleanliness and tidiness are the same as yours, you may start with, "Go clean your room," or "Go clean up the kitchen," with the knowledge that once they start the task they will do it by mutually acceptable standards. However, if you want a room cleaned and your children have a different standard of cleanliness, be as specific as possible in telling them, step by step, what they are to do. For example, our experience shows us that a parent who wants a bedroom to be properly cleaned may need to start with a rule such as this:

"This morning and every Saturday morning, strip the old sheets off your bed and put new sheets on. Dust all your furniture until the dust is gone. Vacuum the carpeting until all I can see is carpet. And take your clothes to the laundry room to be washed."

A few weeks later, the parent can and should start to say with confidence, "Go clean your room, now, and every Saturday morning." The child will know that even though the parent is being more general in stating the rule, he must go to his room, take the old sheets off the bed, put clean ones on, vacuum the floor, dust the furniture, and take his clothes to the laundry room.

After a few more Saturdays, a parent should be able to say, "Please go clean your room now," because the child's experience will be that even though the parent is being polite and general, he still has to go to his bedroom, make the bed, vacuum, dust, and take his clothes to the laundry room—if the parent has been consistent in clearly stating the rule and effectively following through to make sure that the child obeys the rule.

Eventually, you won't have to say anything. The child will begin to enforce the rule on his own.

5

How You Got Out of Control: Ineffective Follow-Through

Human beings (including children) prefer doing things in their own way, in their own time, and given an option, will sometimes do as they please.

If you don't effectively follow through and enforce your own rules, are your children likely to follow through and enforce them on themselves?

Children spend years learning to manipulate parents to get their way. If a two-year-old is told "no" when he asks mama for a candy bar, but daddy says, "yes," the child not only gets a candy bar, but also is encouraged to play parent against parent again. If a three-year-old discovers that mom sometimes gives in and lets her have her way when she throws temper tantrums, she not only gets her way, but also, mom is destined to endure temper tantrums for years to come. If a thirteen-year-old tells her parents she will run away from home if she doesn't get to date her sixteen-year-old boyfriend, and her parents capitulate and let her go, their future will be full of threats to run away. Worse yet, if after years of capitulating to threats of running away, her parents stand up and say "no" to one of her demands, she may feel compelled to run away to show them she really means business.

Kids use what works to get their way—not because they are mean, rotten, nasty, or foul tempered, but simply because they are human beings. Like the rest of us, they want the freedom to do as they please. When children discover that their parents can be manipulated, manipulations are what parents get.

To regain control of your children's problem behavior, you must be able to effectively follow through and enforce your rules. What follows are the most common manipulations used by children and the steps you can take to counteract them.

ARGUING

I was in a large shopping center on a Sunday afternoon as the mall was closing. A young family that had been watching ice skaters in a rink adjoining the mall got up to leave along with the rest of us. Their little boy, who couldn't have been much more than three years old, wanted to stay. His father, seeing that he wasn't following the rest of the family called to him, "John, let's go." The little boy ignored him. Dad repeated his demand, "Let's go."

The boy turned and yelled, "No!"

The father, obviously irritated at this public confrontation, walked to his son and said, "Don't tell me 'no'. When I say we're going, we're going!" The little boy stared at the ice skaters, mute. "Do you hear me?" yelled the dad.

"I want to watch the ice skaters!"

"I don't care what you want. It's time to go."

"No ..."

The ensuing argument lasted almost five minutes, as that three-year-old manipulated—and controlled—his father to watch the ice skaters for an extra five minutes.

Arguments, for our purposes here, are not discussions, negotiations, or an attempt to arrange a meeting of the minds. They are a challenge of wills: Parent against child, and child against parent. Arguments are angry, sometimes vicious, and all too often violent. But if you argue with your children even though you don't want to, take heart; your prayers are about to be answered. In addition to learning why kids argue, you are going to learn how you can stop arguing. And if you were to learn nothing more from this book than how to stop arguments, would your home not be a more peaceful and pleasant place to live?

There are four good reasons, from a child's point of view, to argue with parents: (1) delay, (2) cooling off, (3) wearing the parent down, and (4) power.

Delay. If you are a child who doesn't want to do homework, who would rather watch television than take out the trash, who would prefer polishing your fingernails to cleaning your room, and you can get your parents to argue with you, have you not put off for the entire length of the argument those tasks you've been avoiding?

Cooling Off. Some children will build an argument ... to such an extent ... and get so angry ... that they can't take it any more. They stalk out of the house instead of doing the chores or homework they were supposed to do.

Wearing the Parent Down. Most parents are very familiar with this technique: The child tries repeatedly, and with real tenacity, to keep arguing ... arguing ... arguing ... until the parent, tired and exhausted, finally says something like, "All right, all right, you want to live like a pig? Live like a pig. See if I care." At that point, the child stalks out angrily, chores undone, with a big smile on the inside of his face.

Power. One of the central themes of this book has to do with human beings wanting to be in control of their lives. That goal is nowhere more evident than in arguments where parents really don't want to argue, yet find themselves trapped in arguments with their children. If parents don't want to argue with their children, yet find themselves arguing, who is in control, parent or child? From your experience, are there children who argue just for the sake of getting parents under their control for the duration of the argument?

There is a simple solution: *Never argue with a kid!* You can't win, but a child can. There's a payoff for kids in just getting their parents to argue with them. So, unless you *want* to argue, don't do it. Instead, deflect the argument.

DEFLECTING ARGUMENTS

Arguments have rules. As soon as you defend yourself, the child—by the rules governing arguments—has the right to defend himself against your attack; where, in turn, you get to defend yourself from his attack; until one or both of you give up. But you needn't do that. You don't have to defend yourself against your children's arguments, or try to convince them that you're right and they're wrong.

You are about to get two powerful words that cut through any argument. Coupled with your clearly stated rule, you will find that these words help you to focus on your mandatory behavior rather than on the argument.

The words are "regardless" and "nevertheless" (or their synonyms, "be that as it may," "nonetheless," "that is not the issue"). Only use your argument deflectors once or twice. Then effectively follow through, if a rule is to be complied with "now," and see that the children do as they are told; or if you are merely stating a rule for future behavior, parry their argument with your deflectors, and either walk away or send the child away, letting the child have the last word.
For example:

CHILD: "Billy gets to stay out until ten o'clock on school nights."
PARENT: "Regardless, be home at eight tonight."
CHILD: "That's not fair."
PARENT: "Regardless of whether it's fair or not, be home at eight o'clock if you wish to go out. I'm not going to discuss it further."
CHILD: "Mom, you—"
PARENT: "Go to your room until you're through arguing."
CHILD: "I'm not arguing."
PARENT: (Escorts child to his room without further discussion.)

CHILD: "Everybody else smokes dope."
PARENT: "Regardless, never smoke dope."
CHILD: "You and mom drink booze. I don't see why I can't."
PARENT: "Regardless of what mother and I do, don't drink any alcohol until you're 21 years old."

CHILD: "Dad wouldn't make me do it."
PARENT: "Regardless, sit down and do your English homework now."
CHILD: "You think you know it all! You're so smart."
PARENT: "Regardless of what I know or how smart I am, you may not go to a party without responsible adult supervision."

CHILD: "I'm sick of hearing the word regardless."
PARENT: "Nevertheless, do the dishes now."

Discuss, share, and talk as much as you like, but never, never, argue with your children. Instead, practice deflecting arguments. Your children have taken years to learn how to get you to argue with them. They know the looks, they know the stances, they know the words that set you off. And if you don't practice deflecting arguments to the point of not arguing, you will probably find yourself continuing to argue.

Starting today, keep thinking "regardless" and "nevertheless." The more you practice and use them, the fewer arguments you will have.

PARENT VS. PARENT

Mom is awakened by the noise of her husband's car coming up the driveway. Six hours earlier, after he left work, he'd called to say he'd be home within two hours. Angry and resentful, she's ready for him.

On the way to participate in another inevitable argument with his wife, dad looks in on Billy, his fourteen-year-old son, and finds an empty bed.

In the bedroom, before dad can ask about Billy, mom, in a well-rehearsed, irritating tone demands to know, "Where in the hell have you been? I've been worried sick! You didn't even have the courtesy to give me a call and tell me you were going to be late."

"I called you," he says.

"At six o'clock you called me and said you'd be two hours late. That was six hours ago. It ticks me off that you don't have the consideration to call again and tell me you're going to be even later."

"Dammit, I lost track of the time! Being late is not one of the cardinal sins, you know. By the way, where's Billy? If you're such a great mother, tell me where your son is!"

"What are you talking about?"

"I walked by his room and he's not there. Where in the hell is he? You've been here all night!"

"Yes, I've been here all night, while you spend your time with that fast crowd you run with!"

"Who I hang around with is none of your business. If you had one-tenth the consideration and warmth my friends do, I'd spend more time with you."

"That's a bunch of crap! I make a good home. I don't carouse or run around or get drunk."

"Are you accusing me of running around? Just who am I running around with? Ellen, our sixty-year-old bookkeeper? Or Betty, the nineteen-year-old clerk? Or do you think it's one of your friends? Come on. Talk. You think you've got something on me. Prove it!"

The fight will typically go on for thirty to forty-five more minutes. Mom and dad will get angrier and angrier as the argument becomes a frenzied attack on character, parentage, and sexual proclivities. But where is Billy, their fourteen-year-old son? And during their arguments, who cares?

The most effective loophole kids use to get their way is rarely created by children at all. It stems from the anger and antagonisms, resentments, or general lack of cooperation between parents. If mom says, "Don't drink alcohol as long as you live in this house," and dad, not saying anything, rolls his eyes and casts a loud sigh to show his displeasure at mom's "petty" rule, there is no rule against their son's drinking. If mom and dad have two standards of behavior for the same rule, there is no rule, which means the child gets the option of setting his own rule, good or bad.

A classical type of parental conflict is seen in the "good guy/bad guy" game, where one parent takes the child's side against the other parent. We worked with one family several years ago that played a truly inspired game of "good guy/bad guy."

Fourteen-year-old Jenny spent most afternoons in verbal combat with her mother. Their arguments were prolonged and angry. Several times each afternoon, Jenny's mom would give different versions of "just wait till your father gets home," and when dad walked in the front door, his wife would unleash all of her frustrations and anger on him.

"She's been a little bitch all afternoon. She won't listen to a thing I say. It doesn't matter that I'm her mother. It doesn't matter that she owes me respect. She put me down, called me names, and refused to help in the littlest bit around the house ..." And mom would continue for five to fifteen minutes, demanding that dad "do something!"

Dad, fed up with this nightly confrontation, took mom at her word and started doing something. Each afternoon he'd pick up a newspaper on his way home from work. He'd walk in the house, and as soon as his wife would start to yell, he'd say, "I can see she's been a problem for you today. I'll be glad to handle it, dear." And he'd take Jenny and newspaper to her bedroom, close the door, and sit on her bed and start to read, while his daughter, standing by the door, would slap her hip, yelling, "No! Daddy, no! That hurts! You're always taking her side ... quit hitting me ... you're hurting me!"

Everybody was satisfied with this arrangement. Mom thought Jenny was getting the devil beaten out of her. Dad didn't have to listen to mom's moaning, groaning, and complaining. And Jenny thought it was the greatest scam ever pulled. She could do virtually anything she wanted against her mom, and dad would back her up.

Another form of "good guy/bad guy" occurs when one of the parents becomes a protector. Dad may try to protect the children from mom's "pettiness," or on the other hand, mom may try to protect the children from dad's anger and wrath. Or a parent may attempt to compensate for a spouse's alcoholism or the "unreasonableness" caused by a nervous breakdown.

Any time parents are in conflict over the rules of behavior for their children, those rules are optional. Obeying is left to the discretion of the child. There are, however, some simple steps you may take to minimize this problem.

Solution 1

Fill in the appropriate columns below with the specific mandatory rules you want your children to obey. Note: Duplications are fine. Make your list as complete as space will allow.

Mom's Rules	*Dad's Rules*
_____	_____
_____	_____
_____	_____
_____	_____
_____	_____
_____	_____
_____	_____
_____	_____
_____	_____

Now support this entire list of behaviors. Mom's and dad's rules become household rules with each parent actively supporting—or at least not undercutting—the other's rules. And when one parent believes strongly in a rule and the other doesn't, the rule's "supporter" should have the primary task of enforcing the rule, with the knowledge that his or her spouse will help, if necessary.

Solution 2

If you are adamantly opposed to some of the rules as they stand in Solution 1, then attempt to compromise. If mom believes the children should be home on school nights no later than six, for instance, and dad thinks seven is a more reasonable time, 6:30 p.m. sounds workable. Or if dad wants the children's rooms "picked up" and cleaned seven days a week, and mom thinks Saturday mornings are often enough, Tuesdays, Thursdays, and Saturdays seems like a very nice compromise.

Solution 3

There are few things in this life more frustrating and emotionally distressing to a child than being in a home where parents are trying to enforce conflicting rules. If parents don't agree on the rule, it doesn't exist; so if you can't come to a mutually satisfactory compromise on a rule, eliminate it. Make it completely discretionary with the child.

Solution 4

No marriage can exist without give and take. If you find that you can't agree or compromise on several of the basic behaviors required of your children, the problems you are experiencing aren't with your children's behavior, but with your marriage. You need to see either a marriage counselor or an attorney.

LYING

Edie's mom threw her purse on the table, turned the television off, stood over Edie, her fifteen-year-old daughter, and said, "The school called me at work to tell me you'd cut three more classes."

"I didn't cut. I went to every class," lied Edie.

"Then why would the school say that you did?" asked Mom, wanting to believe in Edie's truthfulness.

"They don't like me."

"What have you been doing to make them not like you?"

"Nothing. Nothing at all."

"It must be something. People won't dislike you because of nothing. Now, what have you been doing?" asked mom, getting even angrier.

Edie stood up, her anxiety no longer allowing her to sit as her mother stood above her, and said, "That's just like you. You never believe anything I say."

"Don't talk to me that way, young lady. You keep a civil tongue in your head. If you don't start to grow up ..."

An argument would typically build from this point to where Mom would start to cry and run to her room.

Lying is one of the best ways to divert parents from their complaints about the child's behavior to "safer" issues, and eventually to an argument that the child will attempt to control (not necessarily win—just control). Edie was quite good at changing the subject from cutting classes, to people not liking her, to her mother's not trusting her, to an angry argument. She took control with a lie.

Some parents are so concerned about children being truthful that they lose sight of their objective: to control the behavior about which the child is lying. And many kids take full advantage of that fact.

Seventeen-year-old David stumbled, staggered, and almost fell through the front door. It was one o'clock in the morning. His mother hulked before him saying, "You've been drinking again."

David, trying to maintain his equilibrium, wavered only slightly as he said, "I have not!"

"Don't stand there and lie to me! I can smell it on you. You stink of whiskey. Now admit it! You've been drinking."

David, having practiced this routine for years, slurred out, "No I haven't."

"Do you take me for a fool? Do you think I'm blind, deaf, and stupid?" asked his mom, feeling more and more helpless.

David finally staggered off to bed, leaving his mother without a confession. At no point did she tell him not to drink.

Lying isn't a problem behavior. It is a manipulation used to hide or obscure real misbehavior. Every time you concentrate on the lie instead of on the misbehavior hidden by the lie, you reduce both your control over the immediate situation and the strength of your demand that the misbehavior be stopped. And if you think about it, wouldn't you rather have a child who doesn't steal or sell dope than one who is truthful about his thefts and dope dealing?

Many times it is very important for you to know the truth, but if the children won't give it to you, if they "stonewall" it, as a recent President of the United States did, you must go, as did the United States Senate, to where the truth lies. Let's look back on Edie and David, and see how their mothers could have handled the situation and maintained control.

Edie's mother threw her purse on the table, turned the television off, stood over Edie and said, "The school called me at work to say that you cut three more classes."

"No I didn't."

"I hope that's true, but let me remind you that you are never to cut another class again," said her mother firmly.

"You don't believe me. You think I cut those classes," replied Edie with a touch of indignity on the edge of her voice.

"Edie, I'll be glad to go to school with you tomorrow and talk to each of those teachers who reported you missing."

Edie paused, looked at her mom, and said, "That's okay. I'll go to class."

Edie's mom merely repeated the rule that she was not to cut class. She was prepared to go to school to seek out the truth, if necessary. She maintained control over the entire dialogue with Edie. Neither of them became angry, and mom got her point across.

David stumbled and almost fell through the front door. His mother hulked before him and said, "David, you're not to get drunk or drink alcohol as long as you live in this house."

"I haven't been drinking and I'm not drunk," slurred David.

"Regardless of your condition or what you've been doing, I'm telling you the rule on drinking. And I'll repeat it for you. Don't drink booze of any kind as long as you live in this house. Now go to bed. I'll talk to you in the morning."

David, not wanting to give up the fight that easily, tried one more time, "But I haven't been drinking."

"We're not talking about whether you've been drinking. Good night. I'll talk to you in the morning."

This time David's mother kept control. She didn't demand a confession. She didn't argue. She simply stated her rule against David's use of alcohol, and she may wish to repeat that rule for David as soon as he is sober.

Never demand a confession from a child. Instead, ask for the truth, and if the child doesn't give it to you, go looking for it. On those occasions when there is no way to determine whether or not the child is telling the truth, simply state your rule and drop the inquisition.

SWEARING

Bobby was sitting at the dining-room table. His school books were sitting beside him. He was supposed to be doing an English assignment, and he had done everything in his power to get out of it. He had tried to start an argument, but his father had told him to be quiet and keep doing the homework. He procrastinated and refused to work, but his mother came in and read part of the reading assignment to him. He told both his mother and his father how dumb he was. They said, "Regardless of how dumb you may be, do your English assignment now."

Out of frustration, because this was the first time in a long time he had been required to do homework, he decided to use his ultimate weapon, the "F" word. And when his mother came in to make sure he was working, he stood up, threw his textbook down, and said, "You fuckin' bitch! I hate your guts!" And just as he planned, it worked. His mother, shaken by that hateful outburst, slapped him across the face and said, "Don't you ever speak to me that way again!"

"Oh, that felt good didn't it bitch? You enjoy hurting me," said Bobby, escalating the argument as he determinedly took control of the situation.

Mom, out of frustration, lashed out, trying to strike him as he simultaneously taunted her and bounced away from her flailing fists. This horrible scene ended when dad walked in, knocked Bobby to the floor, and told mom that Bobby's doing homework wasn't worth this price.

There are times, certainly, when a child's swearing is the issue parents should address. However, in the situation above, just as with children's lies and arguments, parents need to maintain control. Let's replay Bobby's homework scene with mom maintaining control. When his mother came in to make sure he was working, he stood up, threw his textbook down and said, "You fuckin' bitch! I hate your guts!" This time, however, mom stood her ground. She picked up the book and said, "Regardless of my sex habits or parentage, sit back down and do your English. Let's see, you were on chapter five. Do you need help with it?" But Bobby wasn't about to give in that easily and tried again.

"You goddamn bitch! Leave me alone," said Bobby, using anything to get mom off the track.

"I'm not going to leave you alone—not before the homework is done. Now sit down and start working on chapter five. Do you have any questions about it? Or do you want me to start reading to you again?"

Bobby, determined to go all the way, said, "You can read but I'm not going to listen," and put his hands over his ears.

Mom opened the book and started to read aloud. Approximately five minutes later, Bobby took his hands down, looked at her sullenly, and said he would finish it on his own.

Once the homework assignment was completed, mom and dad reiterated the family rule against swearing by taking Bobby aside and in their best "no nonsense" voices telling him, "don't ever, ever, swear at us or anyone else again."

Keep in mind that you have priority behaviors. If you devote time and energy to getting a child to do chores or homework, you don't want to lose it all over a few bad words. Deal with the profanity after you get the first task accomplished. Don't be distracted.

LEAVING

Paula, fifteen years old, was a big girl who intimidated her mother. She simply walked out whenever she wanted to do something her mother said "no" to, or snuck out of her bedroom window at night. And while Mom may have yelled and screamed in the house, and even down the street on occasion, Paula's experience was, "I can get by with this," and she kept doing it. As a consequence, she was heavily involved in drugs and sex (she'd had an abortion). Her former boyfriend, in addition to selling dope, was also a small-time burglar. Paula was unusual in that she didn't argue with her mom. She figured, why bother to argue with someone who doesn't have the power to stop you from doing what you want to do.

Mom, after attending our workshops—with Paula—had a neighbor bolt Paula's bedroom window shut so that she couldn't sneak out of the house at night. (Of course, she prepared an escape plan so Paula wouldn't be trapped if fire erupted.) And she bought a piercingly loud doorknob alarm for Paula's bedroom door.

During the following month, Paula attempted repeatedly to remove the bolts from her window but was unsuccessful. And on three occasions, she attempted to subvert or overtly challenge the alarm on her bedroom door. On each occasion, alerted by the alarm, mom reached the front door before Paula and physically blocked it.

On another night Paula repeatedly set off the alarm, hoping to provoke her mom into giving up. Instead, her mother placed a sleeping bag in front of Paula's bedroom door, removed the alarm, and spent the night. It has been almost a year since Paula sneaked out or left the house without permission. In less than three weeks, her mother regained control at home.

If your children sneak out at night or just blatantly run out the door to avoid having to comply with your rules, do everything in your power to stop them. Lock windows and doors (but always have a fire escape plan and smoke alarms). If necessary, put your body in front of the door to stop them (if they assault you, read the next section, Violence). And if despite your good efforts, they still manage to get out, let them know that any time they leave the house without permission, you, your spouse, and whomever else you can enlist in this effort will be out to bring them home.

VIOLENCE

Rick wasn't quite fifteen years old when his father died. He took it very hard. He started abusing narcotics and alcohol. He became involved in the "punk music" scene and called himself a punk. He had his hair cut in a punk style and dyed orange. He started wearing swastika armbands and purple high-top tennis shoes, along with the rest of the paraphernalia associated with punk. He was especially enthralled with the violence associated with punk and used it repeatedly against his mother.

Rick was his father's only child, and dad had taken Rick's side, right or wrong, against everyone and everything, including mom. On several occasions each year, dad had gotten so drunk and mean that he beat up Rick's mother. The boy grew up believing that mom, and all women, were bitches, nags, and shrews who were never satisfied. For a year and a half after dad's death, Rick beat up his mom. He gave her black eyes, bloody noses, bruises, and welts any time she stood in his way. On several occasions, he threw whatever he had in his hands at her, including kitchen knives.

Less than two weeks after enrolling in our parenting workshops, she began to assume control in her own home. At our suggestion, she enrolled in a judo course. (Judo and aikido are martial arts that are truly self-defensive. They aren't used to maim or injure an assailant.) We also encouraged mom to set up a system for fast protection if Rick became violent before she mastered a few judo techniques: In case Rick got to the telephone before she could get to it, as he had done previously, she told her neighbors that if she yelled, they were to call the police immediately.

Two weeks after enrolling in a five-day-a-week judo program, mom found Rick in the parking lot of a punk club she had placed off limits, and told him to get in the car. He was angry and embarrassed and threw a punch at her face. But applying her new knowledge of judo, she grabbed his arm, pulled him off balance, slammed her knee against his groin, pushed him into the car, closed the door, and drove off.

For the first time in her life, mom had stood up to a male assault. That was nine months ago. Rick is no longer a punk. His orange hair has returned to a very nice brown. His punk junk has been trashed. And he hasn't even tried to attack his mother in almost seven months. For the first time in his life, he and his mother are actually sharing affection. He not only lets her give him hugs, he willingly hugs her back.

If your teenage children are physically violent with you, stop them. Pushing, shoving, or yanking you to get out of the house are just as much a crime of battery as a punch in the nose. Call the police and/or enroll in a self-defense course if necessary.

The majority of parents physically assaulted by their children are attacked at the end of a violent argument. Reaching their breaking point, they haul off and hit the child, and the kid hits back. If you don't argue or hit your children, it is unlikely that you will find yourself in a situation where your children assault you.

PUNISHMENT

It is ironic that punishment, long thought to be a parent's tool to manipulate children, is frequently used by children to manipulate parents. A child willing to take your punishment has the option to do as he pleases. For instance, if your fifteen-year-old knows that he will be grounded on any weekend for coming home late during the week, he may weigh Wednesday night's party, where he knows there will be girls and beer, against the weekend, where he has no plans, and say, "Yeah, it's worth it," and perfectly willingly take your consequences. The manipulation of parental punishment can also be extended to take control of a whole household.

Several years ago, we worked with parents who wanted Tony, their five-year-old, to pick his toys up and put them away when he was through playing with them. Nothing they had done succeeded in getting him to pick up his toys. They had enrolled in a Parent Effectiveness Training course where they learned to "problem solve" the situation, and he'd agreed to pick up his toys. And Mom bit her tongue for weeks as the clutter accumulated throughout the house. Shortly thereafter, they set up a behavior system that rewarded Tony when he picked up his toys and punished him when he didn't. But since he wouldn't pick up his toys, he never got a reward. And since he was willing to take his punishment, he never had to. Finally, they took him to a psychologist who suggested they use "logical consequences" and allow him to learn that if he wouldn't put his toys away, he wouldn't be able to always find them the next time he wanted to play with them. With well-founded skepticism, the parents again watched the clutter accumulate throughout the house, and what they saw was not a boy who was learning a lesson, but a five-year-old who threw temper tantrums when he couldn't find a particular toy.

Just before they came to us, they had an experience that shocked them. Mom told Tony to pick up his toys and he refused to do it. Dad, angry and frustrated, grabbed Tony and gave him a good smack on the bottom. Tony immediately went into a defensive stance—knees bent, fists clenched, staring straight ahead, ready for the next blow. And it came. Thirty-one-year-old dad, seeing a five-year-old stand up to him and not knowing what else to do, hit him even harder. Tony was almost knocked over by the blow, but he went right back into his defensive stance and waited for the next one. And it came. It came so hard, with so much anger and frustration, that he was thrown against the wall. He was hurt—physically and emotionally. Tears welled in his eyes, but he wouldn't give dad the satisfaction of letting them flow. And he stood up, hobbled to his dad, and squatted back down, bottom extended, ready for the next blow.

Tony controlled that house. He was willing to take any punishment in order to do things his way, and he helped his parents feel angry, frustrated, guilty, and helpless; a perfect position for a child who wants to have his own way at any cost.

Rarely is punishment consistently effective in changing behavior. More often than not, it makes the child angry and resentful. And rather than concentrating on what they are or are not supposed to do, they think about how mean, unfair, and unjust you are.

The day after mom and dad enrolled in our program, Tony was required to pick up his toys. His mother took him to each toy, told him to pick it up, and bent down to force his hands around it and make him put it where it belonged. He put every toy in the house away that day. And since mom told him she would do the same thing every time it was necessary, the next time he was told to pick them up, he did it all by himself—because he believed he had no choice.

If punishment succeeded at changing behavior, we wouldn't have to keep using it. We would need fewer prisons, fewer police, and the criminal courts could almost be shut down. It is ironic that the people punished most often in our society are the ones most likely to keep misbehaving.

Don't punish. Instead, effectively follow through.

6

How You Got
Out of Control:
Inconsistency

Human beings (including children) prefer doing things
in their own way, in their own time, and given an
option, will sometimes do as they please.

*Are your children likely to be consistent in obeying rules that you
aren't consistent in enforcing?*

B. F. Skinner, one of America's foremost psychologists, conducted tests
forty-odd years ago using pigeons, and developed the theory of motivat-
ing behavior through what he called scheduled or partial reinforcement.

He divided his pigeons into three separate groups. One group was
rewarded with pigeon "treat" every time it did a certain trick. The
second group was never rewarded for doing the trick. The third group of
pigeons never knew when doing the trick would get them their treat.
Skinner found that the first group of pigeons would frequently get bored
and stop after they ate their fill. He found that the second group
wouldn't do the trick at all ("Just because we're pigeons doesn't mean
we're stupid, buster"). But the third group of pigeons, who never knew
when pushing a button would earn their treat, kept pecking and pecking
and pecking to see if this was the time they'd get what they wanted.

Human beings aren't that different. In situations similar to Skinner's tests, human pigeons in Atlantic City and Las Vegas, who are
inconsistently rewarded with payoffs, repeatedly pull levers, roll dice,
take cards, and choose numbers or colors to see if this is the time they
will win, even though their experience tells them they will probably give

the casino more money than it gives them. There is a reward most human beings want even more than money: To be able to do what we want to do, when we want to do it. And when we are "rewarded" by inconsistently getting our way, we tend to keep pushing to see if we can get our way again.

If you have a fourteen-year-old son who is watching television rather than doing his homework, and you have to tell him three times to get him to do it, his experience tells him that two times out of three, "I don't have to do it yet." He has been "rewarded" twice, and he'll keep pushing to see if he can avoid doing the homework.

A sixteen-year-old truant who can cut classes for four days before the school notifies his parents of his truancies has found, at the very least, that four times out of five he can cut school successfully.

A thirteen-year-old girl who has to be told six times before she makes her bed and picks up the clothes off the floor knows that five times out of six she doesn't have to obey the rule.

Children whose experience says, "I don't have to obey that rule yet," will, like Skinner's pigeons and their featherless cousins in the casinos, persistently push the limits to see if this is the time they can "win"—get their way. We have found that *the best way to encourage children to misbehave is to inconsistently give them the option to do so.*

ANGER, INCONSISTENCY, AND THE IRRITATION SCALE

Inconsistency alone, as you probably know from your experience, produces anger. If you have to tell a child four times to get him to take out the trash or feed the dog or do the homework or mow the lawn just once, you get angry because you have to tell him ... and tell him. And finally, you explode before he does what he is told to do, if he does it at all. The child, on the other hand, hears you as a raging mouth that never stops and is never satisfied. He knows from his experience that he doesn't have to perform the task—yet. And he won't, if he doesn't want to, until you clearly make it mandatory and let him know he has no choice.

In most families, parents and children can accurately graph their irritation, anger, and resentment—as parents nag, harp, needle, wheedle, peck, and pounce on their children, who have to be told repeatedly before doing the "few measly things" assigned to them.

The family situation graphed below is a classic example of parents and kids getting angrier and angrier with each other as the father attempts to get his children to do the dishes. You may not have to look too closely to see yourself in this situation.

DADS, KIDS, AND DISHES

Dad stands six feet tall and weighs over 200 pounds, and it takes him three, four, and five times each night to get his two teenage daughters and teenage son to do their after-dinner chores. Stepmom, who's been in the family only three years, weighs less than 130 pounds, and barely reaches five-foot four, only has to tell them one time to do the dishes, and they do it. Unfortunately for dad, mom works evenings, and the responsibility of making the kids do their chores falls on him.

On most evenings, mom prepares the evening's meal, puts it in the oven, and goes to work. Dad and the kids eat around six o'clock. Dad usually finishes first and goes into his garage workshop. The kids get up a few minutes later to watch television. After twenty to forty minutes, dad, on his way to the bathroom or kitchen, typically walks by the kids and says, "Don't forget to do the dishes tonight," and gets a chorus of, "Okay."

1. Is it likely that kids who prefer watching television to doing dishes will get up at this point and do the dishes? *No. It's clearly optional.*
2. Did dad clearly direct the children to do the dishes *now? No.*
3. Did dad effectively follow through and see to it that they do the dishes *now? No.*
4. Is dad being consistent in getting them to do the dishes or is he going to have to tell them to do it again? *He will have to tell them again.*

Where are dad and the kids on the Irritation Scale?

MILD AND AMIABLE	DAD KIDS	ANGRY AND RAGING

On his second trip through the house, dad sees that the kids are still watching television and says, "Hey guys, you've got chores to do. Let's get busy." One of the kids usually turns and says, "Aw, Dad, we just want to watch the end of this. Can't we please? We'll do them as soon as this is over."

"All right, but as soon as that's over, get in and do your chores."

"Okay, we will." And dad leaves the room.

1. Is it likely that kids who prefer watching television to doing dishes will get up at this point and do the dishes? *No. It's clearly optional.*

2. Did dad clearly direct the children to do the dishes *now? No.*
3. Did dad effectively follow through and see to it that they do the dishes *now? No.*
4. Is dad being consistent in getting them to do the dishes or is he going to have to tell them to do it again? *He will have to tell them again.*

Where are dad and the kids on the Irritation Scale?

MILD AND	DAD	ANGRY AND
AMIABLE	KIDS	RAGING

After another twenty to forty minutes, dad walks through the house again. He notices that no dishes have been done and that all three kids are still watching television. "Dammit, you're supposed to be doing those dishes!"

Barry, the fifteen-year-old boy, or one of his sisters normally turns to dad and says, "You said we could watch this."

Dad isn't sure if they have switched channels or not. He thought they were watching a different program, but he's the kind of father who wants courtroom proof before he accuses the kids of wrongdoing. In his gut, however, he knows that they're putting one over on him and says, "All right, but so help me, as soon as that's over get your butts in that kitchen and start doing those dishes!"

"We will! At least give us a chance to watch this in peace!" says Barry or his sisters, adding, "You said we could."

1. Is it likely that kids who prefer watching television to doing dishes will get up at this point and do the dishes? *No. It is clearly optional.*
2. Did dad clearly direct the children to do the dishes *now? No.*
3. Did dad effectively follow through and see to it that they do the dishes *now? No.*
4. Is dad being consistent in getting them to do the dishes or is he going to have to tell them to do it again? *He will have to tell them again.*

Where are dad and the kids on the Irritation Scale?

MILD AND	DAD	ANGRY AND
AMIABLE	KIDS	RAGING

Twenty to forty minutes later, at least two hours after he first started telling the kids to do their dishes, dad walks through the front room again. The dishes aren't done; the kids are still watching television—and they've switched channels.

"That's it. I am sick to death of this. I give you an inch and you take a mile. Every night it's the same crap! Now get up, get in that kitchen, and do those dishes right now."

"We were just getting ready to," say the kids. "You should at least give us a chance before you start yelling and screaming."

"Give you a chance! I give you a million chances and you take advantage of every damn one of them!" says dad angrily, escorting all three kids into the kitchen where he again demands, "Clean these dishes, now!"

1. Is it likely that kids who prefer watching television to doing dishes will get up at this point and do the dishes? *Yes. It's mandatory at this moment (but the children view the rule as optional most of the time).*
2. Did dad clearly direct the children to do the dishes *now? Yes.*
3. Did dad effectively follow through and see to it that they do the dishes *now? Yes.*
4. Was dad consistent in getting them to do the dishes? *No.*

Where are dad and the kids on the Irritation Scale?

MILD AND		DAD	ANGRY AND
AMIABLE		KIDS	RAGING

DAD, KIDS, AND DISHES, PART 2

The first night after attending the Back In Control Workshop, dad walks into the front room after dinner, turns the television set off, and reaches down to help Barry get up as he looks at his daughters and says, "Ladies, join your brother and me in the kitchen." He then escorts all three of them into the kitchen, where he says, "Clean it up right now and do a good job just like you would for mom." Note: Some parents will have to be more specific about defining the tasks that go into making a "clean" kitchen. In this family, once they start, the children clean the kitchen by standards acceptable to the parents.

The kids looked at him, dazed and bewildered, and started doing the dishes.

1. Did dad clearly direct the children to do the dishes *now? Yes. It is mandatory.*
2. Did dad effectively follow through and see to it that they did do the dishes *now? Yes.*
3. Was dad consistent in getting them to do the dishes? *Yes. He did it the first time, and if he continues to do so, the children will see the rule as mandatory.*

Where are dad and the kids on the Irritation Scale?

MILD AND	DAD		ANGRY AND
AMIABLE	KIDS		RAGING

Which method—mandatory or optional—is more likely to produce a positive relationship between parent and child? *Mandatory.*

Which method—mandatory or optional—will give the kids more "good" time to watch television? *Mandatory.*

Based on your experience with your children, which method—mandatory or optional—will they choose if you don't enforce the rule as a mandatory? *Optional.*

Most parents clearly state their rules—at times—and effectively follow through—at times—to make sure that their children obey those rules. The biggest obstacle parents face is being inconsistent. And believe me, your kids will do everything in their power to help you be inconsistent. If you're too busy, too angry, too tired, too hassled, or just plain unwilling to follow through and enforce your own rule, you aren't in control. The child has the option to behave as he or she pleases; and, if you decide to enforce the rule at a later date, you will find that you have an even more difficult time getting the child to obey it than you would have had the first time. Remember, the best way to encourage children to misbehave is to inconsistently give them the option to do so.

To regain control of your children's misbehavior, you must consistently enforce your rules.

7

Getting
Back in Control
by Word and Deed

If you don't clearly state your rules, whose interpretation of those rules are your children likely to use, yours or theirs?

If you don't effectively follow through and enforce your own rules, are your children likely to follow through and enforce them on themselves?

Are your children likely to be consistent in obeying rules that you aren't consistent in enforcing?

This chapter contains examples of directions to use and steps to take in setting mandatory rules for your children's behavior. The directions are clear, brief, and precise. Use them as they are, or alter them to suit your own needs. But remember, the more words you use, the less clear your directions are likely to be.

The steps recommended below for effective follow-through have been successfully used by thousands of parents in our private and Juvenile Justice Programs. They are designed to restore parental control. Some of them are time-consuming and energy-sapping, but if you are to overcome months or years of a child's experience that says, "I can do what I want to do and you aren't going to stop me," then you must give her new experiences to the contrary.

If, however, you aren't willing to consistently follow through, and you're the only one who can judge whether your rules are worth enforcing or not, don't nag, punish, manipulate, or beg to get your children to obey a rule that you aren't willing to enforce. It comes down to a simple choice: Either it's *your rule*—mandatory—and you are going to enforce it. Or it's *the children's rule*—discretionary—and you will leave enforcement of the rule to their discretion. Either solution will bring peace to your home.

BEDWETTING

Sample Directions

"Get up when your bladder is full and use the bathroom."

"Get up at_____(specific time) and go to the bathroom every night."

Effective Follow-Through

Withhold liquids two or three hours before bedtime, and require that the children urinate before they go to bed. And since the idea is to have them empty their full bladders, either set your alarm clock based on when they normally urinate so you can wake them up and take them to the bathroom before they wet the bed, or buy an "alarm sheet"—Sears sells them as "Wee Alert"—that will wake them as they start to wet the bed. It is essential that children be awakened so they associate the pressure of a full bladder with waking up and using the bathroom. If you have a difficult time awakening them, either squirt a fine water spray in their faces or wave an amonia-soaked cotton ball under their noses until they wake up.

Consistency

Do this every night, until the children consistently start to get up and go to the bathroom on their own. If an "accident" occurs after they start having dry nights, repeat the process. If you are unwilling to be consistent in enforcing this rule, give your children the discretion to wet the bed.

Comments

Paradoxically, many anxious bedwetters compel themselves to wet the bed out of fear that they will wet the bed. One twenty-year-old bedwetter with whom we worked was engaged to be married and fearful of a wet wedding night. She had gone to sleep most of her life thinking, "I know I'm going to wet the bed, I know I'm going to wet the bed," programming herself to do the very thing she didn't want to do. But that process can be reversed, as it was with our twenty-year-old client, who started going to bed at night thinking, "I will wake up when my bladder is full and go to the bathroom." Within a few days, and with her mother's help in doing what we suggested above, she was dry at night and her wedding night wasn't marred by a urine-soaked bed.

CHORES AND HOUSEHOLD RESPONSIBILITIES

Sample Directions

"Take out the trash now."

"Go pick up your clothes and put them in the clothes hamper. Make your bed. Dust the furniture until the dust is off. And vacuum the floor until all the lint and cat hair is picked up. Now."

If the child's standard of cleaning a bedroom is the same as your's, "Go clean your room right now."

If you are attempting to establish a continuing rule that the child will obey on a regular schedule, you may wish to say, "Go do the dishes right now, and do them every day immediately after dinner."

"The lawn is to be mowed every Saturday. Start no later than ten o'clock in the morning. Go mow the lawn now." (If the child's standards for a well-maintained lawn are different from yours, you may wish to specify exactly what she is to do each time she mows the lawn until her work on the lawn is consistent with your specifications.)

Effective Follow-Through

When you want a child to do a chore, make sure he does it at the time you want it done. At the very least, don't walk away until the child is up and starting to do the chore, which is all most parents have to do. If he is stubborn, go one step further. For instance, if he is watching television and you want him to take out the trash "now," if he doesn't want to, turn off the television and take him to the trash. If necessary, escort him out to the trash can where it is to be dumped. Or, as some parents have done, take the trash to him, put it in his lap, and escort him out to the trash can if necessary.

If your children's speed in doing chores makes snails, tortoises, and stubborn donkeys look fast, and they won't speed up on their own, help them finish the tasks at a reasonable speed. If they are vacuuming very, very slowly and they don't respond to your directions to speed up, put your hands on theirs, theirs on the vacuum cleaner, and make them go at your pace. If they are so slow that the cleanser they pour in the sink dries before the sink is completely scrubbed, and they don't go faster after you tell them to, put your hands on theirs, theirs on the scrub cloth, and clean the sink promptly. Do this with each necessary task to help procrastinators and slow-motion marvels speed up.

It is not necessary to follow through if the child will do the chores as directed.

Consistency

Every time you want a particular chore or household job done, tell the child specifically what to do and when to do it, and until she starts to do it on her own, follow through to see that it is done. Don't tell a child to do a chore during this catch-up period (while you are regaining control) unless you are going to follow through and enforce it the first time you tell her to do it. If you find yourself returning to tell a child a second time to do something once, she knows from experience that half the time she doesn't have to do what you say, and she is likely to keep pushing and pushing to see if this is the time she can do it her way.

Comments

You will find that getting your children to do their share around the house or yard will be much easier if you schedule a program of chores rather than periodically telling them to do varying household jobs. Specify what they are to do and when it is to be done. For example, if you tell a child each Saturday morning, "Get out of bed and clean up your room now," there is no continuing requirement that he clean his room other than when you tell him to do it. However, if you say, "Clean your room by ten o'clock every Saturday morning. Get up and clean it now," the child will know, if you are consistent, that he must clean his room by ten o'clock every Saturday morning. Eventually, he will get up on Saturday mornings before ten o'clock and clean the room on his own.

If you are unwilling to consistently enforce this rule, give your children the discretion not to do chores.

CURFEW AND PUNCTUALITY

Sample Directions

"Be home at_____(specific time) tonight."
"Be home by_____(specific time) on school nights and_____(specific time) on weekends."

Effective Follow-Through

There are three ways to make sure children are home on time.

1. If you can't trust a child to come home promptly, it is perfectly all right to say, "No, you can't go out."
2. If you know where your children are, either call them on the telephone and tell them to come home immediately, or go and get them and bring them home.
3. If you want them to go out, but from experience you know they may not stay where they have permission to be, or that they may not come home on time, you may want to go with them.

We worked with a family whose fourteen-year-old daughter would go out on a Friday night date with her boyfriend and not return until Sunday night. (I personally think fourteen-year-old children are too young to date, but her parents wanted her to have the social experience of dating.) I asked dad, who had been in our program months before to stop his daughter's truancy, how he'd gotten his daughter to go to school. And he said, "I followed your advice: I told her very clearly that she had to go, and when she didn't believe me, I took her to school and walked her from class to class. She believed me then. She hasn't cut a class in more than six months."

"Keeping that in mind," I asked, "can you think of a way to make sure that she comes home from her Friday night dates on Friday?"

Dad looked at mom, at me, and then at his daughter, and said, "Well, I suppose I can go with her." And dad did. That night she was home before her curfew for the first time in months. Her boyfriend, Chuck, never asked her out again, and for the six months that we followed up on the family, she was home from her Friday night dates on Friday.

If your children have a history of coming home late, or of not staying where they are supposed to be, keep them in, or go get them, or go with them. After a suitable period of time—and you're the best judge of what that time is—start giving them a little freedom to see how they handle it. If they come home from school promptly and they didn't used to, you can give them freedom to stay out longer. If they go to a friend's house and stay there as they are supposed to (check to make sure they are there), you can start giving them more freedom to go to other friends' houses. In general, give them the freedom their behavior justfies. But if they test your rule by coming in late or not staying where they are supposed to be, tighten up.

Consistency

If it is a mandatory rule that they be home at a certain time or be at a specific place, follow through each time they want to go out until they start to enforce the rule on themselves.

If you are unwilling to consistently enforce this rule, give your children the discretion to come home when they please.

DRUG AND ALCOHOL ABUSE

Sample Directions

"Never use drugs or narcotics of any kind unless they're prescribed by a doctor."

"Never smoke marijuana again."

"Never use hard narcotics."

"Don't drink booze now or until you're twenty-one."

"Do not drink alcohol as long as you live in this house, and no, you may not leave until you're eighteen."

"You may have wine with dinner in our home, but until you're twenty-one, don't drink alcohol anywhere else."

Effective Follow-Through

If your children have a moderate to serious problem with alcohol or drugs, it is essential that you know where they are, who they're with, and what they're doing. If someone calls on the phone, find out who it is. When the children leave the house, know where they're going. Get addresses, phone numbers, and names. Follow up: Use the phone or, when appropriate, go and check to make sure that they're where they're supposed to be and that they're not using drugs and/or alcohol.

If you cannot depend on your children to avoid drugs and alcohol when they're out of the house, they need to stay either with you or under other responsible adult supervision. They should be occupied with rewarding and fulfilling activities. They should be in school every day doing their assigned work. They should be home at night with the family, sharing family life and doing their homework. If there is a time gap between when school gets out and when the rest of the family comes home, fill it with a vocational educational program; a part-time job (under responsible adult supervision); after-school athletics, dramatics, journalism, or music; or a community program operated through responsible organizations such as churches, Y's, or parks and recreation departments.

Unfortunately, many schools ignore student drug or alcohol abuse. You need to know whether your children's schools do a good job keeping drugs and alcohol off campus. Go to the school and look around. Talk to kids and teachers. If you look closely and talk to enough people, you will get a candid impression of what's going on at the school. Do not, under any circumstances, rely solely on the word of the principal that the school is drug or alcohol free. If you find a principal who admits they have a problem with drugs and alcohol, don't accept his word that the school can't do anything more than they're doing about it, because they can.

If the school is lax and your children have a history of drug or alcohol abuse, you may need to take them to school, search their lockers periodically, see who they associate with at lunch, and make sure that they don't use or exchange drugs or alcohol. Our experience shows that school administrators frequently acquire new motivation to combat children's drug and alcohol abuse when parents come on campus regularly.

Know what's in your child's room. A child who abuses drugs or alcohol has no right to privacy. If you don't know anything about drugs, call your local police agencies, juvenile probation departments, or drug diversion programs. Even better, locate a parents' anti-drug-and-alcohol program within your community. Within the last few years, these parent groups have sprung up across the nation. They can tell you what to look for and where to look for it, and give you support from other parents on the same crusade.

In addition to drugs and alcohol, look for the paraphernalia associated with it, including syringes, "bongs," hash pipes, cigarette rolling papers, and empty booze bottles. Also look for and remove posters, magazines (such as *High Times*), jewelry, and clothing that promote the use of drugs or alcohol. Make your children's immediate environment drug and alcohol free.

Never let your children attend teenage parties unless you have complete confidence in the party's sponsor or accompany your child yourself.

Consistency

Know where your children are, who they are with, and what they are doing until you are confident they are enforcing your rule against drug and alcohol abuse on their own.

If you are unwilling to be consistent in enforcing this rule, either give your children the discretion to use drugs and alcohol, or place them in a residential treatment center and hope for the best.

Comments

Severe cases of drug and alcohol abuse may be best initially treated in a residential treatment center where the child will stay for a few days to several months, but don't count on treatment programs to cure the problem. Their typical success rates run somewhere between 30 and 40 percent. You must, as soon as the child is back home, follow the steps set out above if you wish to prevent further drug or alcohol abuse.

I cannot overstate the harm done to children by drugs and alcohol. I have known too many children who have died, and too many alcohol- and drug-devastated families to think of children's drug and alcohol abuse as anything but an abomination. There are no redeeming reasons for children to use narcotics or alcohol.

FIGHTING WITH SIBLINGS

Sample Directions

"Quit, stop, don't ever_____(whatever they're doing to each other)."
In that most sibling fighting stems from ill-tempered words, you may wish to set a rule preventing not only physical assaults but also the words that provoke them. If so, you may wish to say, "Be quiet now, and don't argue with each other again."
"Don't ever call your brother/sister_____or any word or expression like it."
On the other hand, it could be that you don't mind if the children fight, but you just don't want to hear it. If that's the case, you may be comfortable saying, "Don't argue or fight when you're around me."
"Don't argue or fight in the house. If you're going to fight, do it outside or in the garage."

Effective Follow-Through

Step in and break up the fight, the argument, or the word assault, and separate the children from one another. Send them to their respective rooms or to different parts of the house, or keep them with you, until they have cooled off. If you're in the car, pull off to the side of the road, demand they stop, and don't start the car up again until they are quiet. If they merely aren't to fight in the house, send or escort them to where they may fight.

Consistency

Repeat the process every time you see or hear the offending behavior.

If you are unwilling to consistently enforce this rule, give your children the discretion to fight and name-call as they please.

FIGHTING WITH OTHERS

Sample Directions

> "Never hit anyone."
> "Never hit anyone except_____(specify your exception)."

Effective Follow-Through

Unless your children develop a pattern of fighting, your demand alone is frequently enough to get them to stop. But if a pattern does exist, follow through and prevent the fights based on your experience as to when they most likely occur—at school, after school, in the neighborhood. And don't allow your little fighter to be unsupervised until he has learned that you really mean he must not fight.

Consistency

Make your demand every time you know of a fight, and consistently follow through to stop the fighting when a pattern develops.

If you are unwilling to consistently enforce this rule, give your children the discretion to fight as they please.

PEER PRESSURE

Sample Directions

> "Never associate with_____(name the people—adults and/or children—with whom they are not to associate)."
> "You may be with_____(name the person) only_____(name the location and/or time)."

Effective Follow-Through

Know where your children are, who they are with, and what they are doing. Depending on your experience with your children's behavior, check by phone (less effective) or in person (far more effective) to ensure that they are where they are supposed to be. And if you cannot trust the child to obey the rule, don't let her out of the house unsupervised.

Consistency

Make your demand every time it's necessary, and effectively follow through until the child demonstrates that she will enforce the rule on her own.

If you are unwilling to consistently enforce this rule, give your children the discretion to see whomever they please.

Comments

If your children do things against your rules when they are with their friends, you may want to curtail, reduce, or supervise their mutual activities. If the misbehavior involves narcotics, alcohol, stealing, truancy, or other delinquent acts, you may wish to strive for a 100 percent ban against their co-delinquents. On the other hand, if your children, when they are with their friends, "forget" where they are supposed to be or when they are supposed to be home, or if they get into neighborhood mischief somewhat short of delinquency, you may want to either supervise their time together or limit their associations to those times and circumstances when they aren't likely to get into trouble.

Experience has shown us that as parents act to stop drug and alcohol abuse, stealing, truancy, and similar offenses, friends who participated in these acts will start to shun and avoid the children who are now acting straight and sober.

Never "put down" your children's friends. Explain any restriction you may place on their time together in terms of misbehavior, not of character. The last thing you want to do is to put your children in a situation where they feel compelled to defend a badly behaving friend.

RUNNING AWAY

Sample Directions

"Don't leave this house without permission, ever!"
"Get home right now and never leave again without permission."
"Don't run away from home ever!"

Effective Follow-Through

Inasmuch as most children who run away from home stay within a few miles of their homes, if you start looking for them through their friends and their friends' parents, you will almost always find them in a short time—a few hours to a few days. Looking gives you more than just the opportunity to find your child. The grapevine will let her know that you are looking, and that's important. If you don't know any of your child's friends, go to school and talk to teachers, counselors, administrators, or anyone else who might know the names of her friends and associates. Even if you come up with only one name, that person can probably lead you to someone else, who may lead you to someone else, who can lead you to your child.

If the child has been missing for several weeks or longer and you have had no word from him, you might want to hire a private investigator, and without question, file a missing persons report with the local police department.

Consistency

Every time your child runs away, track him down, bring him home, and give him a clear demand that he not run away again. If you are consistent, the running away will become less and less frequent and eventually stop.

If you are unwilling to consistently enforce this rule, give your children the discretion to live where they please.

Comments

Children run away from home for a number of reasons. Sometimes it's just to get their way. Other times it's because they don't feel accepted or loved at home. But unless their home is horrible, their chances of finding something better on the outside is slim.

Our experience in southern California shows that better than 90 percent of the runaways remain in their communities and stay with friends, acquaintances, or exploiters. Of the 10 percent who leave the community, about half leave the state heading north or east. The remaining 5 percent, including boys, sell themselves on southern California's streets of sex.

If someone is hiding your child and will not return her, you may need to involve the police. If so, keep in mind that laws passed over the last several years have in some jurisdictions prohibited or discouraged the police from apprehending runaways. Therefore, if you call for police assistance to help get your child out of a home where adults or other children are harboring her, instead of saying you want help to bring your runaway home, say, "I have located my son/daughter, who is a runaway, at____(give the address). I am going to get him/her and there is probably going to be a big fight. I'd like an officer to help keep the peace." You will probably get an officer to help you.

SCHOOL PERFORMANCE— IN CLASS

Sample Directions

"Do everything the teacher assigns to you, every day."

"Do everything assigned to you by the teacher, and if you don't understand it, ask the teacher for help."

If behavior problems in the classroom are causing poor achievement, "Don't_____(whatever the child is doing) in class."

Effective Follow-Through

If your directions from home aren't enough, and your contact with the teacher (personally, through school progress reports, or with the help of *The Back In Control School Achievement Book*) shows that your child is not performing or behaving properly, go to class with him on the day following any problem that teachers either can't or won't handle by themselves. While you are in the class, direct the child to do what is required, and make sure he does it.

Consistency

Repeat this as often as necessary. The more consistently you follow through, the more your children will believe they must obey your rules about school behavior and performance.

If you are unwilling to consistently enforce this rule, give your children the discretion to do as they please in class.

Comments

If you want your child to do well in school, take the steps necessary to ensure that success. Some teachers, like parents, have lost control; others have given it away. If your children are in such a situation, or if they have a history of school-related problems, make their teachers' optional rules into your mandatories. This requires a weekly, and perhaps a daily, progress report informing you of how well your children are performing and behaving in class. If the school is geared to help you with this, use its system. If it isn't, or if its system isn't appropriate to your needs, either use *The Back In Control Assignment Book*, or adapt the book's format to your specific needs.*

*See Appendix B.

SCHOOL PERFORMANCE—
HOMEWORK

Sample Directions

"Do every homework assignment and turn it in on time."

"Unless the teacher specifically tells you to do an assignment in class, show me everything assigned to you to do before it is due."

If you are making them do a specific assignment at home, "Do your English on page 81 now."

"Now do math problem 18."

Effective Follow-Through

If at all possible, at approximately the same time each school day, arrange a place for the child to study that is quiet and well lighted, with enough space to write.

If your children's experience tells them they don't have to do homework, it will almost assuredly require your immediate physical presence to see that they do it. If they are being highly resistive, involve yourself in the homework. Ask questions, suggest sample answers, and follow through until it is done—even if the children are belligerent, combative, and resentful to find that they, of all people, are going to have to do homework.

To find out what their home assignments are, use the school's weekly or daily progress reports. If that is inappropriate, use *The Back In Control School Achievement Book*, or make up your own daily or weekly progress reports from the sample included in Appendix B.

It is vital that your children know that you will follow through and make them do the homework that has been assigned to them. The more consistent you are about this, the less work you will have to do.

Consistency

Follow through every day. If your children are fairly good about doing their homework, make sure that they are up-to-date on their assignments at least once a week.

Make them believe, by your words and actions, that they actually have to do all of their assignments.

If you are unwilling to consistently enforce this rule, give your children the discretion to not do their assignments.

Comments

You may find it interesting that many teachers never specifically assign "homework." Instead, they give a reading assignment that is due tomorrow, or a book report that is due a week from Wednesday, or they remind their students to review for Friday's test. The word "homework" is frequently not used. So when you ask your children, "Do you have homework?" they interpret your question literally and say "no." If they carelessly speed through their English assignment in history class, and their history assignment in math class, and their math assignment at lunch, from their point of view, the "homework" has been done. See, it's obvious isn't it: They don't have "homework."

SEXUAL MISBEHAVIOR

Sample Directions

"Don't have sex with anyone until_____(the time or circumstance you believe to be appropriate).

If sexual relations are okay, but motherhood isn't, "Take this birth control pill every day or as required by the prescription."

Effective Follow-Through

Do not allow them to date until they are emotionally mature enough to handle boy/girl relationships. A good rule of thumb is somewhere around fifteen or sixteen years old.

If your goal is to prohibit your children in engaging in sex acts, you need to take steps to reduce their freedom to do so. Discourage single-couple dates. Encourage dates to school events, proms, special dances, plays, and concerts. Set a reasonable curfew for dates, and know where your children are going. At times, they may wish to go to a restaurant or ice cream shop at the end of a date, which should be within acceptable limits. They should not be alone with dates or probable sex partners in other people's homes. And unless you are willing to accompany them, do not allow them to attend teenage parties that are either unsupervised or supervised by someone you don't know.

If, on the other hand, sexual behavior is discretionary and pregnancy isn't, you need to take steps to make sure your girls are taking their birth control pills. (Chemical contraceptives are the only effective means by which parents can make sure their sexually active children don't get pregnant, as it is unlikely that parents will be there to make

60

sure the boy puts on a condom or the girl inserts a diaphragm or spermacides.)

Consistency

Enforce your curfews and dating restrictions each time your children go out on a date. Anytime you have reasonable doubts about where they are or what they are doing, check on them.

Or if you are seeing to it that your girls use birth control pills, consistently follow through each day and see that they take them.

If you are unwilling to consistently enforce this rule, give your children the discretion to have sex in a manner of their own choosing.

Comments

In days past, when families were together both physically and emotionally, children could bear children and still raise them to become responsible adults because they had help from their parents, grandparents, aunts, and uncles. Today, a child raising a child out of wedlock or in a very young marriage frequently doesn't have the consistent contact with her parents that is necessary to help her raise a child. Teenage parents—because of their inexperience, immaturity, and ignorance of child rearing—frequently become frustrated, angry, and resentful; and they take their painful emotions out on the child. My strong advice is to discourage and do your best to prevent children's sexual experimentation until you believe they are mature enough to accept the responsibility of parenthood, or until you are ready to assume the role of surrogate mother or father to help your child raise her child.

STEALING

Sample Directions

"Don't steal anything from anybody, ever!"
"Never take anything that doesn't belong to you without the owner's permission."

Effective Follow-Through

To stop your children from stealing, you need to know where they are, who they are with, and what they are doing. Get phone numbers, addresses, and names. Check to make sure they are where they are supposed to be. Make sure they are in school during the school day, and that their time is constructively occupied when you are not around. If they have an established pattern of stealing, they need to be supervised by responsible adults until they demonstrate that they will no longer steal.

Be aware of your child's possessions. Prohibit "found" articles from being in the house. Inquire and fully check out "borrowed" items if you have any doubt about their ownership.

If your child "forgets" where he got an item, or who he "borrowed" it from, or doesn't have a receipt verifying its purchase, donate it to a charitable cause. Don't let children profit from stolen or possibly stolen items.

Consistency

Every time you have reason to believe that your child has stolen something, give her a clear, direct demand that she not do it. Effectively follow through by taking the stolen item from the child and continuing to monitor her whereabouts and activities until she appears to be obeying your rule against stealing.

If you are unwilling to consistently enforce this rule, give your children the discretion to steal.

Comments

Stealing is one of the simplest things for parents to stop. Whether children are shoplifting, burglarizing, or in the extreme, robbing people, parents can put a permanent stop to the behavior.

TEMPER TANTRUMS

Sample Directions

"Calm down and quit throwing things, now."
"Calm down now."

When trying to stop a temper tantrum, do your best to remain as cool and calm as can be. Don't scream and yell. Remain as calm as possible, and never give in to a temper tantrum.

Effective Follow-Through

For young children, if the tantrum is mild, you may wish to send them to their room until they are through. But if the children are older, or if the tantrum is violent and causing harm to the children themselves, to other people, or to the house, intervene. Remain calm, but do everything you can do to stop the behavior. If you have to sit on the child, lay on the child, hold the child as close as possible, do so. If you need help, call for assistance from neighbors or relatives, and if necessary because of violence, the police.

Let the child know that you will let him go as soon as he calms down. If he starts again, repeat the process until he has calmed down.

Consistency

Never let a tantrum pay off. Do not give in and allow children to have their way. If you have decided that your children are no longer to throw tantrums, every time one starts, demand in a calm but firm voice that it stop. If necessary, follow through as described above and stop it.

If you are unwilling to consistently enforce this rule, give your children the discretion to scream their heads off.

Comments

Human beings, especially children, throw temper tantrums either because they are frustrated and angry or because they have learned that tantrums are an effective way to get people off their backs. Our experience shows us that the majority of temper tantrums arise from arguments, and that if you just don't argue, the temper tantrums will stop.

TRUANCY

Sample Directions

> "Go to every class, every school day, and stay there until you are officially released."
> "Never cut class again."

Effective Follow-Through

Take the child to school—from class to class (with period-cutters)—on the day following the truancy. If you need help to drag the child out of bed and off to school, call on friends, school officials, police, or anyone willing to help. If everyone declines, don't give up, just work harder.

If you cannot get same-day notification of your children's truancies, either use *The Back In Control School Achievement Book* or make up your own daily attendance sheet from a sample in Appendix B. Have the child obtain daily teacher verification in every class where truancy is a problem. Explain the problem to every teacher, and ask each one to provide written verification of your child's attendance until you are confident your child is going to class every day. We have never had a teacher refuse to cooperate. Some have resisted or been resentful, but parents who were tactful, and willing to talk to the school administration, if necessary, have always gotten cooperation. If you don't, and your experience has shown that the school isn't consistent about adequate notification of your children's truancy, consult an attorney. You may have the makings of a good lawsuit.

Consistency

Every time your child cuts a class or is truant, repeat your demand and follow through to make sure that she is in class the next day.

Thousands of southern California's most school-hating truants and their families have been referred to our workshops, and all parents who followed our suggestions stopped their children's truancy.

The all-time record for Back In Control parents consistently escorting children to school and from class to class is shared by a forty-seven-year-old widow and a forty-one-year-old divorcee. Each took three days, over a five- to six-week period, to get her son (one seventeen, one fifteen) to every class, every school day, for the rest of the semester.

If you are unwilling to consistently enforce this rule, give your children the discretion to be truant.

Comments

Truancy today is not Huck Finn and Tom Sawyer taking off to raft down the Mississippi. It's ignorance—children falling behind, giving up in their studies, not learning to develop habits of completing assignments and getting to assigned places on time. Truancy allows children to be unsupervised during the school day, and it is directly linked to drug and alcohol abuse, emotional distress, and daytime crime.

In big-city school systems truancy is characterized by period-cuts, where children are allowed either to stay on campus relatively undisturbed by adult supervision or to come and go as they please. This often leads to all-day cuts, where the child doesn't come to school at all. If schools won't do their part in keeping your children on campus and in class, you must do it yourself.

8

Sharing Your Love

Even though most parents want to share love with their children, it's hard to be loving and affectionate with a child who habitually misbehaves, who must always have his way, or who relentlessly and argumentatively pushes until his parents give in or explode. But it is just as hard for a child who hears and feels angry arguments, yelling, denunciations, and punishments to be loving and affectionate with his parents.

If you and your children find yourselves frequently sharing anger and resentment instead of love and affection, reach out—whether they wish to be reached for or not—and pull them back into the heart of the family. Start by enforcing your mandatory rules. Since well-behaved children are much easier to love and appreciate than those who aren't, just having them obey your mandatories will make them more pleasant and lovable. And if you reach out to your children with the goal of sharing love, they will start to share their love with you.

EXPRESSING APPRECIATION

When your children comply with your mandatory rules, thank them, or sincerely acknowledge the pleasure of having their cooperation, as appropriate. Act as though the child were doing of her own volition what you told her to do.

If you have to escort her to the kitchen to pick up the trash can, and on out to the street for the weekly trash pickup, thank her when the job is completed. If he finished a very difficult homework assignment under your close supervision, tell him how proud or pleased you are that he did it. Even when children unwillingly comply with parental demands, they still need to hear parental appreciation and support for obeying the rule.

ATMOSPHERE

Begin and end each day with words expressing love, caring, and belonging:

> "Good morning," in a cheery voice.
> "It's good to see your smiling face," (but only if the face is smiling).
> "Hi, how are you this morning?"
> Other "good morning" greetings that seem appropriate to your family, even if the previous day and evening were horrible.

End the day the same way.

> "Good night, sleep tight, don't let the bedbugs bite."
> "I really appreciate the things you did for me today," (if, indeed, the child has done something worthwhile for you today).
> "Good night, I love you"—even if the day has been a bad one.

You set a tone of love and caring in your home by starting and ending the day saying good things to one another. Encourage your children to respond, but don't give up if they don't. And keep reaching out to them with your words of love. Eventually—and it won't be too long—your children will return them.

BEING TOGETHER

Spend time together as a family even if you can spare only a few minutes a day. Play games, watch television, go to the movies, go out to eat, go for walks. And if your children's school achievement is less than it could be, work on their homework with them. Share the events of the day. Talk about things that interest both of you, and things of special interest to the child alone. Do something fun together. To the best of your ability, make your home a loving, caring place to be. Whether the children want to be there or not, even if they are ornery, angry, and hostile, bring them into the family.

NO ISOLATION

All of us need privacy at times, but when privacy becomes isolation, the child withdraws from the family and the family from the child. So don't let your children spend an excessive amount of time by themselves or away from the family. A child who spends virtually every night behind his bedroom door listening to his stereo, watching television, or out of the house with his friends, needs to have that time reduced—but not necessarily eliminated—so he may spend more time with the family.

TOUCHING

If you aren't already doing it, share hugs and kisses with your children. However, if you have exchanged too much anger and resentment, and the best you can offer one another are hateful hugs and cold kisses, start slowly and simply—with touching. A warm, gentle touch on an arm, knee, hand, or shoulder can go a long way toward restoring a caring parent/child relationship.

It is much easier to accept a demanded behavior from a parent who shares love and affection than from one who nags, yells, screams, and condemns. And the more you consistently reach out to your children, the easier it will be to get them to obey your rules.

9

Arthur, Ken, and Emma Rejoined

ARTHUR—THE CHORE HATER

Arthur's mom, on the night following the first Back In Control Workshop, came home to find Arthur watching television, as usual, his chores undone. This night, however, things were different. Jean didn't yell, scream, nag, or argue. When the show Arthur was watching concluded, she turned off the television and said, "You've several things to do. I've made a list of your afternoon chores, and because I need to fix dinner, the first thing that has to be done is the kitchen." And in a firm but calm voice, she said, "Go clean the kitchen right now."

But Arthur, who never gave in easily on anything, challenged his mom. "That's not fair, I wanted to watch 'MASH.'"

Mom stood her ground and said, "After your chores are done, you will have all evening to watch television. Go do the dishes now."

Arthur saw that his mom wasn't leaving, wasn't arguing, wasn't angry, and wasn't going to back down. He knew she meant he had to do the dishes, and he got up and washed them. When he finished, she complimented him on the good job he had done, got out the vacuum cleaner, and said, "Vacuum the living room floor completely." She periodically looked in from the kitchen, where she was cooking dinner, to see that he was doing a good job.

When he finished, she walked him to his bedroom and said, "Make your bed, and pick up your clothes, including those on the bottom of the closet, and put them in the clothes hamper."

"But I'm going to be sleeping in the bed in less than three hours. Why do I have to make it?"

"Regardless of when you go to bed, make your bed now."

"But that's stupid. There's no good reason to make the bed now."

"Regardless of how stupid it may be, make the bed now," replied Jean resolutely.

"No! I don't see any point in making the bed," yelled Arthur, as he avoided the bed and reached down to pick up the clothes his mother had told him to pick up.

After he put his clothes in the hamper, as his mother had told him to do, he gave her a dirty look and said, "You don't have to spy on me, I'm doing what you said."

"I know you are, and I'm very pleased with that." And she stayed and watched him make the bed. He was angry, he was resentful, but he did everything she had told him to do. She hadn't argued, and she remained in control.

Less than two weeks after starting The Back In Control Workshops, Jean started coming home to tell Arthur, "Get busy on your chores right now." And he would get up, turn the television off, do the dishes, vacuum the floor, and start on his homework (the second behavior she had selected to get under control). Arthur was now making his bed in the morning, because as he got up, Jean would go into his bedroom, tell him to make it, and see that he did. There had been no arguments in the home for almost two weeks. The anger and resentment that Arthur had shown when mom first started enforcing her rules was no longer there. And although he was now doing homework each evening, he still had more good free time in which to watch television than he'd had previously, because when he finished his chores and homework, there was nothing for his mother to yell, scream, or nag about.

In addition to enforcing her household rules on chores and homework, Jean thanked Arthur for doing his chores. She told him how pleased she was that he was doing his homework well, even though he wouldn't do it if she didn't make him. She started bringing him juice or hot chocolate as he was getting ready to go to school in the morning, something she hadn't done in years. In the evenings, she made a special effort to say, "Good night," and "I love you," to Arthur and his sister, Melinda. She also insisted that Arthur, Melinda, and she spend time together at least three days a week. They started playing games, visiting together, and going places as a family.

By the end of the month, on most days (but not all), Arthur didn't even have to be told to do his chores. He did them as soon as mom got home. Nor did he have to be told to make his bed in the morning. Again, he did this on his own, although mom did have to check it for quality, and there were times he had to re-do it. But Jean's anger, resentment, frustration, and feeling of helplessness were gone. She was using less effort and getting better behavior. And she and Arthur shared affection and love for the first time in years.

KEN—THE DOPE DEALER

Ken's parents, Barbara and Don, were determined to make Ken and their home drug free. On the morning following the workshop, after Ken went to school, they cleaned out his room. Every poster depicting or glorifying drugs was trash-canned, as were his drug-influenced jewelry, drug scales, rolling papers, stash cans, and most important, his dope. They found six lids of grass, a vial of hash oil, and fifty bindles of white powder. They also found $400 in cash, which they hid in their room.

When Ken came home and saw what had happened, he was furious. "God dammit, do you know what you've done?" he screamed, as he looked through the room to see what they had taken. He kicked a hole in his closet door and yelled, "You fuckin' assholes, you've ruined my life!"

Firmly and calmly, as calm as one could be under those circumstances, Don said, "Regardless of whether your life is ruined or not, never have anything to do with drugs again."

By this time, Ken discovered that they had also taken his money. "What did you do with my money, asshole? I owe it to people who will kill me if it isn't paid!" he screamed.

"All right!" shouted dad, extending his palm. "We want this crap ended. We'll let you pay off the creeps supplying you with dope. But it will be the last time." And he restated his demand. "Do not have anything to do with dope. Don't sell it, possess it, or use it. And don't hold it for anyone else."

In a final effort to rid his home of drugs, Don said, "Now empty your pockets. We want to make sure you don't have any dope."

"I'm not giving you anything! Those fuckers down at the program (Back In Control) think they know it all, but there's no way you're ever gonna get me to stay away from dope. I like it and it's my life. Now leave me alone!"

"Empty out your pockets now!" said his dad firmly.

Ken ran for the door, but his dad grabbed him and wrestled him to the carpet. And while the two of them sprawled across the floor, Barbara emptied Ken's pockets of crumbled five-, ten-, and twenty-dollar bills, four joints, and three bindles of white powder.

As Don left to get rid of the dope, Barbara kneeled beside Ken, who was still lying on the floor, put a shaking hand on his shoulder, and said, "I know you feel we are being mean and hateful, but you have no idea of how much we love you."

The next day mom and dad took Ken to school. They told the assistant principal that mom would be coming to school every day at lunchtime to make sure Ken didn't deal dope or hang around with kids that did.

For that week and several following, Ken had no unsupervised time. He was either at school supervised by school people and his mother, or he was at home. On the evening of the second day of the new program, Ken went with his parents, unwillingly, to return the money he owed his suppliers.

For the next month, Barbara and Don consistently followed through to make sure that Ken was drug free. They checked his room regularly, they searched him, and mom periodically made appearances at lunchtime on campus.

They also set a new tone for the family by spending time together, although for the first couple of weeks it didn't feel like "good" time. At the end of the month, they felt secure enough to allow Ken to have the freedom to have a part-time job after school if he wanted one, or to become involved in after-school activities. He chose a job, and started to work at a Mexican fast-food restaurant.

We followed up on this family for more than six months, and things got progressively better and better. Not only were the parents alcohol free, for, if you remember, they were recently recovered alcoholics, but their son was drug free also. Ken's school grades came up. He started associating with a relatively drug-free group of kids, and was given more and more freedom as his behavior warranted it. However, his parents continued to periodically check his room to make sure there were no drugs. And when he was out of the house, they now knew where he was, and what he was doing.

EMMA—THE TRUANT

Emma, as you may recall, didn't like going to school, and successfully fought her mother to stay in bed in the morning. On the day after attending her first Back In Control Workshop, Betty awakened Emma, saying, "It's 6:30, get out of bed now."

And when Emma replied, "Leave me alone!" mom stepped across Emma, braced her feet against the wall, and pushed Emma out of bed, saying, "Get up, now."

Emma was furious. Her mother had never done this before. "You goddam bitch!" she screamed, "You could have hurt me!"

Not wanting to argue and not needing to, Betty said calmly and firmly, "Get your clothes on, get ready for school now."

"I'm not going to school and you can't make me!"

"I don't care whether you get dressed or not, what's important is that you go to school. If you want to go in your nightie, I don't care. Now either get dressed and go to school, or go as you are."

"Fuck you, I'm not going!"

Betty stuck her head into the hallway and asked Francine, a neighbor and friend whom she had asked to stand by, to help. The two of them literally carried Emma, kicking and screaming, out to the car. Betty brought clothes along in case Emma decided to dress. Francine drove while mom, sitting on Emma in the back seat, was called every insulting, infuriating name Emma knew. But despite the screaming and a good attempt at biting her mother's leg, Emma got to school and decided to get dressed before she left the car.

Emma's parting words as she walked into the attendance office were, "You fuckin' bitch, I hate your guts!" But she spent the day in school.

When mom went to get Emma up the next morning, she found the door locked. After prying the lock open, she saw that Emma had barricaded the door with a dresser. She and Francine pushed against it until it toppled over.

"You fuckin' bitch, I'm not going to go to school!" screamed Emma as her mom and Francine pulled her out of bed, grabbed her clothes, and carried her to the car again. But on that day she put on her clothes and brushed her hair as Francine drove them to school.

That evening Betty removed the door to Emma's bedroom, and the next morning when she said, "It's 6:30, get out of bed now," Emma got out of bed. And while it is true she got out of bed snarling and saying horrible things, she did obey her mother's rule: She went in on her own and got ready for school. And Francine waved as mom and Emma drove to school.

Betty was very careful each evening to tell Emma how pleased she was that she was getting up and going to school. She told her each night that she loved her, and she arranged a Saturday outing for the two of them, something they hadn't done in months.

By the end of the month, Emma was getting up on her own with only an occasional reminder. She stopped throwing temper tantrums.

She stopped swearing at her mother, and following her mother's lead, she began saying, "I love you."

There were positive benefits at school as well. Not only was Emma attending class every day, but also, as she participated in classroom activities, her teachers reached out to her with encouragement. And after mom saw to it that she did homework, Emma began to get the best grades of her life. Instead of school being a torment, it became a pleasure. And instead of a home full of anger and resentment, Emma and her mom now had a home full of love and caring.

10

A Chapter
for the Kids

WHAT ARE THEY UP TO NOW?

Your parents probably bought this book because they are concerned about what they consider to be your misbehavior. You may not do chores they tell you to do, or they may feel you have to be told too often before you finally do them. Or they may be concerned about school problems, drug or alcohol abuse, stealing, running away, or even worse behavior.

Most of the parents who buy this book argue more than they want to and sometimes, out of frustration and anger, say things they don't mean. This book will help to stop that in your family. Using the book correctly, your parents will learn how to stop arguing, nagging, and yelling. They will learn how to make your home a more pleasant and peaceful place. They will also be encouraged to stop punishing you.

In previous chapters, your parents have been encouraged to deal specifically with changing your behavior, rather than with changing you as a person. After reading this book, your parents will understand, if they didn't already, that *you* aren't the problem, and that they must concentrate, instead, on changing your behavior.

Your parents have been told about the three types of behavioral rules:

1. *Mandatory*—you have no choice but to obey.
2. *Optional*—they think you have no choice, but you have found the means to do things your way.
3. *Discretionary*—your parents give you permission to make your own decisions.

A mandatory rule has three parts: Clear directions—so you know exactly what to do, or not to do; effective follow-through—to show you that you must obey the rule; and consistency. If even one of these parts is left out, your parents don't have a mandatory rule, they have an optional one. For instance, if they don't clearly tell you what to do, you may interpret their directions to your own advantage. If they don't effectively follow through to enforce their rule, it's unlikely, unless you believe the rule is worthwhile, that you will enforce it on yourself. And finally, if they aren't consistent in enforcing their rule, it's unlikely that you will be consistent in obeying it.

Optional behaviors cause anger, resentment, and sometimes violence, because your parents have an expectation that you should obey their rules, while your experience tells you that sometimes you can do things your way. Your parents are upset with you because you break their rules. You're upset with them because they always seem to be picking on you, and may even be punishing you.

However, when your parents require that you obey the mandatory rules (*they* get to decide what's mandatory) and give you the discretion to use your judgment in everything else, your home will be a more peaceful, pleasant, loving place to be.

WHAT GIVES THEM THE RIGHT
TO TELL ME WHAT TO DO?

The answer to that question is simple—*love*. I have worked with thousands and thousands of families, and I've seen that the driving force to get children to do well in school, do chores, be home at a certain time, not steal, or not be involved in drug or alcohol use, is love.

Your parents, almost without exception, want you to be able to "stand on your own two feet." Many of the things they require of you are to help you become a productive, happy adult. Many parents want their children to do chores, not only because the chores need to be done, but also to establish a habit pattern. Then when you leave home, you will be able to cook your own meals, clean up after yourself, keep the mold in the bathroom down to a tolerable level, and keep the clutter in your bedroom down to a point where you can at least find the bed.

Parents, from their experience and their maturity, frequently and accurately see problems where children don't. No kid taking a drink, smoking a joint, or snorting a spoonful of "coke" for the first time sees himself dying in a traffic accident or dropping out of life under the influence of a chemical. But his parents do. And the vision justifiably scares them.

Very few children shoplifting a stereo tape or entering a neighbor's house while the neighbor's at work see themselves in Juvenile Hall or jail, but their parents do. And that idea frightens them too.

Believe it or not, your parents have a very good sense of what's best for you. And while they may be wrong at times, their instincts, more often than not, are absolutely right. Your parents have rules for you because they love you, and while that love may sometimes be hidden beneath yelling, screaming, threats, and punishment, it's still there, and it's working in your best interest.

Appendix A:
Questions and Answers

Q. Won't too many strictly enforced rules cause children to rebel and behave even worse?

A. If that were true, America's young delinquents, incorrigibles, and malcontents would no doubt be led by raging gangs of Mennonite Christians, Black Muslims, and Hasidic Jews, rather than, as is the case, the children of parents who spend little, if any, time supervising their children's behavior.

Q. My children know the difference between right and wrong. Why do they continue to misbehave?

A. If merely knowing the diffrence between "right and wrong" were an effective way of controlling human behavior, one glance at the Ten Commandments would make saints of us all. Your children misbehave because they want to do so, and their experience tells them they are going to get by with it at least some of the time.

Q. You make it sound as if I have to be a dictator. Won't my children hate me?

A. Your children may not like what you do very much at any given moment, but they won't love you less for consistently enforcing your important rules. Inconsistent reinforcement, however, may irreparably harm the love between you.

Q. I do more for my children than I do for myself. Why don't they appreciate what I go through for them?

A. You can't expect your children to appreciate what you're doing for them. They will not truly understand or appreciate your rules, restrictions, and concerns until they become parents themselves. (Yes, your mother was absolutely right when she cursed you with, "Just wait until you have children of your own...")

Q. I want my children to think for themselves. Won't this system stifle them?

A. Human beings are born knowing how to think for themselves, they don't have to be taught. But they do have to be taught to behave properly.

Q. I want to be able to give my children the responsibility of behaving properly without having to force them. Is that unreasonable?

A. No more unreasonable than wanting to lose weight without having to change your eating habits or increasing your physical activity. You are assuming that your children share your perceptions of the world and, using common sense, will come to the same conclusions you do. Children, however, frequently see things differently, and as a consequence, come to different conclusions.

Q. How much freedom should I give my children?

A. As much as their behavior warrants. The better they behave, the more freedom they earn. The worse they behave the less they earn.

Appendix B:
A Daily Plan

DAILY PLAN/DAILY REVIEW
WORKSHEETS

Your children have spent years training you to give them options. They know how to get you to argue, how to wear you down, how to play dad against mom, how to procrastinate, and numerous other means to confuse, distract, and manipulate you to their advantage. To overcome this handicap, and to get Back In Control of your children's behavior, you must practice clearly stating your rules, effectively following through, and being consistent.

This week and each week for the next four weeks, choose a misbehavior that you wish to get rid of from among those listed in Chapter 7. Each day, fill in the clearly stated rule, planned follow-through, and planned consistency on the Daily Plan. Repeat the words of your clearly stated rule aloud until they are comfortable and natural. Review the steps you will take to effectively follow through, if necessary, and to be consistent. Then execute your plan each day until you are in control of that misbehavior. At the conclusion of each day, review your accomplishments in the Daily Review.

Only work on one new mandatory behavior a week. Parents who attempt to regain control of every misbehavior at once frequently find the job overwhelming, and give up. However, by consistently enforcing one new rule each week, you will establish credibility with your child. When you attempt to control a second, third, or fourth behavior, her experience will tell her that she actually must obey those rules. Even better, many children not only obey the mandatories that parents are currently enforcing, but also start to self-enforce mandatories their parents planned to enforce in the future. And if you follow through consistently and continue to enforce your rules, your children will eventually get to the point where they enforce all of your mandatories on their own.

By the end of four weeks, you and your children will have had plenty of practice in the Back In Control system, and you should be able to get them to obey virtually any rule. If you can't —and some families need more than four weeks—keep following the program until you feel in control. Or if a month, six months, or a year or more passes and your children start to misbehave again, go back to the basics. Remember, power belongs to those who use it. If you don't, your children will. And if you aren't clearly stating your rules, and effectively, consistently following through, your children will continue to do as they please.

DAILY ASSIGNMENT SHEET

Use the following daily assignment sheet format to construct your own assignment, attendance, and behavior monitoring system, or use *The Back In Control School Achievement Book.*

CLASS/PERIOD   DATE:_____

_____

Today's Assignments/Due Dates

_____

_____

_____

Test Results and Assignments Returned

_____

_____

_____

Deportment and Attendance

_____

_____

_____

Teacher's Comments and Verification

_____

_____

_____

The Daily Plan

This week's mandatory behavior:_____

My clearly stated rule:_____

_____

_____

_____

My planned follow-through, if necessary:_____

_____

_____

_____

My planned consistency:_____

_____

_____

_____

The Daily Review

1. Did you clearly state your rule as planned? If not, please review chapters 4 and 7.

2. If it was necessary, did you effectively follow through and enforce the rule as planned? If you didn't, please review chapters 5 and 7.

3. Were you consistent? Did you enforce the rule immediately and until it was obeyed? If not, please review chapters 6 and 7.

4. If you were successful, congratulations. If you were not, review the appropriate sections of the book and start again tomorrow. Don't give up! You will succeed.

FIRST WEEK—FIRST DAY

The Daily Plan

This week's mandatory behavior:_____

My clearly stated rule:_____

_____

_____

_____

My planned follow-through, if necessary:_____

_____

_____

_____

My planned consistency:_____

_____

_____

_____

The Daily Review

1. Did you clearly state your rule as planned? If not, please review chapters 4 and 7.
2. If it was necessary, did you effectively follow through and enforce the rule as planned? If you didn't, please review chapters 5 and 7.
3. Were you consistent? Did you enforce the rule immediately and until it was obeyed? If not, please review chapters 6 and 7.
4. If you were successful, congratulations. If you were not, review the appropriate sections of the book and start again tomorrow. Don't give up! You will succeed.

FIRST WEEK—SECOND DAY

The Daily Plan

This week's mandatory behavior:_____

My clearly stated rule:_____

_____

_____

_____

My planned follow-through, if necessary:_____

_____

_____

_____

My planned consistency:_____

_____

_____

_____

The Daily Review

1. Did you clearly state your rule as planned? If not, please review chapters 4 and 7.

2. If it was necessary, did you effectively follow through and enforce the rule as planned? If you didn't, please review chapters 5 and 7.

3. Were you consistent? Did you enforce the rule immediately and until it was obeyed? If not, please review chapters 6 and 7.

4. If you were successful, congratulations. If you were not, review the appropriate sections of the book and start again tomorrow. Don't give up! You will succeed.

FIRST WEEK—THIRD DAY

The Daily Plan

This week's mandatory behavior:_____

My clearly stated rule:_____

_____

_____

_____

My planned follow-through, if necessary:_____

_____

_____

_____

My planned consistency:_____

_____

_____

_____

The Daily Review

1. Did you clearly state your rule as planned? If not, please review chapters 4 and 7.

2. If it was necessary, did you effectively follow through and enforce the rule as planned? If you didn't, please review chapters 5 and 7.

3. Were you consistent? Did you enforce the rule immediately and until it was obeyed? If not, please review chapters 6 and 7.

4. If you were successful, congratulations. If you were not, review the appropriate sections of the book and start again tomorrow. Don't give up! You will succeed.

The Daily Plan

This week's mandatory behavior:_____

My clearly stated rule:_____

_____

_____

_____

My planned follow-through, if necessary:_____

_____

_____

_____

My planned consistency:_____

_____

_____

_____

The Daily Review

1. Did you clearly state your rule as planned? If not, please review chapters 4 and 7.

2. If it was necessary, did you effectively follow through and enforce the rule as planned? If you didn't, please review chapters 5 and 7.

3. Were you consistent? Did you enforce the rule immediately and until it was obeyed? If not, please review chapters 6 and 7.

4. If you were successful, congratulations. If you were not, review the appropriate sections of the book and start again tomorrow. Don't give up! You will succeed.

FIRST WEEK—FIFTH DAY

The Daily Plan

This week's mandatory behavior:_____

My clearly stated rule:_____

_____

_____

_____

My planned follow-through, if necessary:_____

_____

_____

_____

My planned consistency:_____

_____

_____

_____

The Daily Review

1. Did you clearly state your rule as planned? If not, please review chapters 4 and 7.

2. If it was necessary, did you effectively follow through and enforce the rule as planned? If you didn't, please review chapters 5 and 7.

3. Were you consistent? Did you enforce the rule immediately and until it was obeyed? If not, please review chapters 6 and 7.

4. If you were successful, congratulations. If you were not, review the appropriate sections of the book and start again tomorrow. Don't give up! You will succeed.

FIRST WEEK—SIXTH DAY

The Daily Plan

This week's mandatory behavior:_____

My clearly stated rule:_____

_____

_____

_____

My planned follow-through, if necessary:_____

_____

_____

_____

My planned consistency:_____

_____

_____

_____

The Daily Review

1. Did you clearly state your rule as planned? If not, please review chapters 4 and 7.

2. If it was necessary, did you effectively follow through and enforce the rule as planned? If you didn't, please review chapters 5 and 7.

3. Were you consistent? Did you enforce the rule immediately and until it was obeyed? If not, please review chapters 6 and 7.

4. If you were successful, congratulations. If you were not, review the appropriate sections of the book and start again tomorrow. Don't give up! You will succeed.

FIRST WEEK—SEVENTH DAY

The Daily Plan

This week's mandatory behavior:_____

My clearly stated rule:_____

_____

_____

_____

My planned follow-through, if necessary:_____

_____

_____

_____

My planned consistency:_____

_____

_____

_____

The Daily Review

1. Did you clearly state your rule as planned? If not, please review chapters 4 and 7.
2. If it was necessary, did you effectively follow through and enforce the rule as planned? If you didn't, please review chapters 5 and 7.
3. Were you consistent? Did you enforce the rule immediately and until it was obeyed? If not, please review chapters 6 and 7.
4. If you were successful, congratulations. If you were not, review the appropriate sections of the book and start again tomorrow. Don't give up! You will succeed.

SECOND WEEK—FIRST DAY

(Select a new mandatory behavior in addition to continuing to work on last week's mandatory.)

The Daily Plan

This week's mandatory behavior:_____

My clearly stated rule:_____

_____

_____

_____

My planned follow-through, if necessary:_____

_____

_____

_____

My planned consistency:_____

_____

_____

_____

The Daily Review

1. Did you clearly state your rule as planned? If not, please review chapters 4 and 7.
2. If it was necessary, did you effectively follow through and enforce the rule as planned? If you didn't, please review chapters 5 and 7.
3. Were you consistent? Did you enforce the rule immediately and until it was obeyed? If not, please review chapters 6 and 7.
4. If you were successful, congratulations. If you were not, review the appropriate sections of the book and start again tomorrow. Don't give up! You will succeed.

SECOND WEEK—SECOND DAY

The Daily Plan

This week's mandatory behavior:_____

My clearly stated rule:_____

_____

_____

_____

My planned follow-through, if necessary:_____

_____

_____

_____

My planned consistency:_____

_____

_____

_____

The Daily Review

1. Did you clearly state your rule as planned? If not, please review chapters 4 and 7.

2. If it was necessary, did you effectively follow through and enforce the rule as planned? If you didn't, please review chapters 5 and 7.

3. Were you consistent? Did you enforce the rule immediately and until it was obeyed? If not, please review chapters 6 and 7.

4. If you were successful, congratulations. If you were not, review the appropriate sections of the book and start again tomorrow. Don't give up! You will succeed.

SECOND WEEK—THIRD DAY

The Daily Plan

This week's mandatory behavior:_____

My clearly stated rule:_____

_____

_____

_____

My planned follow-through, if necessary:_____

_____

_____

_____

My planned consistency:_____

_____

_____

_____

The Daily Review

1. Did you clearly state your rule as planned? If not, please review chapters 4 and 7.
2. If it was necessary, did you effectively follow through and enforce the rule as planned? If you didn't, please review chapters 5 and 7.
3. Were you consistent? Did you enforce the rule immediately and until it was obeyed? If not, please review chapters 6 and 7.
4. If you were successful, congratulations. If you were not, review the appropriate sections of the book and start again tomorrow. Don't give up! You will succeed.

SECOND WEEK—FOURTH DAY

The Daily Plan

This week's mandatory behavior:_____

My clearly stated rule:_____

_____

_____

_____

My planned follow-through, if necessary:_____

_____

_____

_____

My planned consistency:_____

_____

_____

_____

The Daily Review

1. Did you clearly state your rule as planned? If not, please review chapters 4 and 7.
2. If it was necessary, did you effectively follow through and enforce the rule as planned? If you didn't, please review chapters 5 and 7.
3. Were you consistent? Did you enforce the rule immediately and until it was obeyed? If not, please review chapters 6 and 7.
4. If you were successful, congratulations. If you were not, review the appropriate sections of the book and start again tomorrow. Don't give up! You will succeed.

SECOND WEEK—FIFTH DAY

The Daily Plan

This week's mandatory behavior:_____

My clearly stated rule:_____

_____

_____

_____

My planned follow-through, if necessary:_____

_____

_____

_____

My planned consistency:_____

_____

_____

_____

The Daily Review

1. Did you clearly state your rule as planned? If not, please review chapters 4 and 7.

2. If it was necessary, did you effectively follow through and enforce the rule as planned? If you didn't, please review chapters 5 and 7.

3. Were you consistent? Did you enforce the rule immediately and until it was obeyed? If not, please review chapters 6 and 7.

4. If you were successful, congratulations. If you were not, review the appropriate sections of the book and start again tomorrow. Don't give up! You will succeed.

SECOND WEEK—SIXTH DAY

The Daily Plan

This week's mandatory behavior:_____

My clearly stated rule:_____

_____

_____

_____

My planned follow-through, if necessary:_____

_____

_____

_____

My planned consistency:_____

_____

_____

_____

The Daily Review

1. Did you clearly state your rule as planned? If not, please review chapters 4 and 7.

2. If it was necessary, did you effectively follow through and enforce the rule as planned? If you didn't, please review chapters 5 and 7.

3. Were you consistent? Did you enforce the rule immediately and until it was obeyed? If not, please review chapters 6 and 7.

4. If you were successful, congratulations. If you were not, review the appropriate sections of the book and start again tomorrow. Don't give up! You will succeed.

SECOND WEEK—SEVENTH DAY

The Daily Plan

This week's mandatory behavior:_____

My clearly stated rule:_____

_____

_____

_____

My planned follow-through, if necessary:_____

_____

_____

_____

My planned consistency:_____

_____

_____

_____

The Daily Review

1. Did you clearly state your rule as planned? If not, please review chapters 4 and 7.

2. If it was necessary, did you effectively follow through and enforce the rule as planned? If you didn't, please review chapters 5 and 7.

3. Were you consistent? Did you enforce the rule immediately and until it was obeyed? If not, please review chapters 6 and 7.

4. If you were successful, congratulations. If you were not, review the appropriate sections of the book and start again tomorrow. Don't give up! You will succeed.

THIRD WEEK—FIRST DAY

(Select a new mandatory behavior in addition to continuing to work on the two previous weeks' mandatories.)

The Daily Plan

This week's mandatory behavior:_____

My clearly stated rule:_____

_____

_____

_____

My planned follow-through, if necessary:_____

_____

_____

_____

My planned consistency:_____

_____

_____

_____

The Daily Review

1. Did you clearly state your rule as planned? If not, please review chapters 4 and 7.

2. If it was necessary, did you effectively follow through and enforce the rule as planned? If you didn't, please review chapters 5 and 7.

3. Were you consistent? Did you enforce the rule immediately and until it was obeyed? If not, please review chapters 6 and 7.

4. If you were successful, congratulations. If you were not, review the appropriate sections of the book and start again tomorrow. Don't give up! You will succeed.

THIRD WEEK—SECOND DAY

The Daily Plan

This week's mandatory behavior:_____

My clearly stated rule:_____

_____

_____

_____

My planned follow-through, if necessary:_____

_____

_____

_____

My planned consistency:_____

_____

_____

_____

The Daily Review

1. Did you clearly state your rule as planned? If not, please review chapters 4 and 7.

2. If it was necessary, did you effectively follow through and enforce the rule as planned? If you didn't, please review chapters 5 and 7.

3. Were you consistent? Did you enforce the rule immediately and until it was obeyed? If not, please review chapters 6 and 7.

4. If you were successful, congratulations. If you were not, review the appropriate sections of the book and start again tomorrow. Don't give up! You will succeed.

THIRD WEEK—THIRD DAY

The Daily Plan

This week's mandatory behavior:_____

My clearly stated rule:_____

_____

_____

_____

My planned follow-through, if necessary:_____

_____

_____

_____

My planned consistency:_____

_____

_____

_____

The Daily Review

1. Did you clearly state your rule as planned? If not, please review chapters 4 and 7.

2. If it was necessary, did you effectively follow through and enforce the rule as planned? If you didn't, please review chapters 5 and 7.

3. Were you consistent? Did you enforce the rule immediately and until it was obeyed? If not, please review chapters 6 and 7.

4. If you were successful, congratulations. If you were not, review the appropriate sections of the book and start again tomorrow. Don't give up! You will succeed.

THIRD WEEK—FOURTH DAY

The Daily Plan

This week's mandatory behavior:_____

My clearly stated rule:_____

_____

_____

_____

My planned follow-through, if necessary:_____

_____

_____

_____

My planned consistency:_____

_____

_____

_____

The Daily Review

1. Did you clearly state your rule as planned? If not, please review chapters 4 and 7.

2. If it was necessary, did you effectively follow through and enforce the rule as planned? If you didn't, please review chapters 5 and 7.

3. Were you consistent? Did you enforce the rule immediately and until it was obeyed? If not, please review chapters 6 and 7.

4. If you were successful, congratulations. If you were not, review the appropriate sections of the book and start again tomorrow. Don't give up! You will succeed.

THIRD WEEK—FIFTH DAY

The Daily Plan

This week's mandatory behavior:_____

My clearly stated rule:_____

_____

_____

_____

My planned follow-through, if necessary:_____

_____

_____

_____

My planned consistency:_____

_____

_____

_____

The Daily Review

1. Did you clearly state your rule as planned? If not, please review chapters 4 and 7.
2. If it was necessary, did you effectively follow through and enforce the rule as planned? If you didn't, please review chapters 5 and 7.
3. Were you consistent? Did you enforce the rule immediately and until it was obeyed? If not, please review chapters 6 and 7.
4. If you were successful, congratulations. If you were not, review the appropriate sections of the book and start again tomorrow. Don't give up! You will succeed.

THIRD WEEK—SIXTH DAY

The Daily Plan

This week's mandatory behavior:_____

My clearly stated rule:_____

_____

_____

_____

My planned follow-through, if necessary:_____

_____

_____

_____

My planned consistency:_____

_____

_____

_____

The Daily Review

1. Did you clearly state your rule as planned? If not, please review chapters 4 and 7.

2. If it was necessary, did you effectively follow through and enforce the rule as planned? If you didn't, please review chapters 5 and 7.

3. Were you consistent? Did you enforce the rule immediately and until it was obeyed? If not, please review chapters 6 and 7.

4. If you were successful, congratulations. If you were not, review the appropriate sections of the book and start again tomorrow. Don't give up! You will succeed.

THIRD WEEK—SEVENTH DAY

The Daily Plan

This week's mandatory behavior:_____

My clearly stated rule:_____

_____

_____

_____

My planned follow-through, if necessary:_____

_____

_____

_____

My planned consistency:_____

_____

_____

_____

The Daily Review

1. Did you clearly state your rule as planned? If not, please review chapters 4 and 7.

2. If it was necessary, did you effectively follow through and enforce the rule as planned? If you didn't, please review chapters 5 and 7.

3. Were you consistent? Did you enforce the rule immediately and until it was obeyed? If not, please review chapters 6 and 7.

4. If you were successful, congratulations. If you were not, review the appropriate sections of the book and start again tomorrow. Don't give up! You will succeed.

FOURTH WEEK—FIRST DAY

(Select a new mandatory behavior in addition to continuing to work on the three previous weeks' mandatories.)

The Daily Plan

This week's mandatory behavior:_____

My clearly stated rule:_____

_____

_____

_____

My planned follow-through, if necessary:_____

_____

_____

_____

My planned consistency:_____

_____

_____

_____

The Daily Review

1. Did you clearly state your rules as planned? If not, please review chapters 4 and 7.

2. If it was necessary, did you effectively follow through and enforce the rule as planned? If you didn't, please review chapters 5 and 7.

3. Were you consistent? Did you enforce the rule immediately and until it was obeyed? If not, please review chapters 6 and 7.

4. If you were successful, congratulations. If you were not, review the appropriate sections of the book and start again tomorrow. Don't give up! You will succeed.

FOURTH WEEK—SECOND DAY

The Daily Plan

This week's mandatory behavior:_____

My clearly stated rule:_____

_____

_____

_____

My planned follow-through, if necessary:_____

_____

_____

_____

My planned consistency:_____

_____

_____

_____

The Daily Review

1. Did you clearly state your rule as planned? If not, please review chapters 4 and 7.

2. If it was necessary, did you effectively follow through and enforce the rule as planned? If you didn't, please review chapters 5 and 7.

3. Were you consistent? Did you enforce the rule immediately and until it was obeyed? If not, please review chapters 6 and 7.

4. If you were successful, congratulations. If you were not, review the appropriate sections of the book and start again tomorrow. Don't give up! You will succeed.

FOURTH WEEK—THIRD DAY

The Daily Plan

This week's mandatory behavior:_____

My clearly stated rule:_____

_____

_____

_____

My planned follow-through, if necessary:_____

_____

_____

_____

My planned consistency:_____

_____

_____

_____

The Daily Review

1. Did you clearly state your rule as planned? If not, please review chapters 4 and 7.

2. If it was necessary, did you effectively follow through and enforce the rule as planned? If you didn't, please review chapters 5 and 7.

3. Were you consistent? Did you enforce the rule immediately and until it was obeyed? If not, please review chapters 6 and 7.

4. If you were successful, congratulations. If you were not, review the appropriate sections of the book and start again tomorrow. Don't give up! You will succeed.

FOURTH WEEK—FOURTH DAY

The Daily Plan

This week's mandatory behavior:_____

My clearly stated rule:_____

_____

_____

_____

My planned follow-through, if necessary:_____

_____

_____

_____

My planned consistency:_____

_____

_____

_____

The Daily Review

1. Did you clearly state your rule as planned? If not, please review chapters 4 and 7.
2. If it was necessary, did you effectively follow through and enforce the rule as planned? If you didn't, please review chapters 5 and 7.
3. Were you consistent? Did you enforce the rule immediately and until it was obeyed? If not, please review chapters 6 and 7.
4. If you were successful, congratulations. If you were not, review the appropriate sections of the book and start again tomorrow. Don't give up! You will succeed.

FOURTH WEEK—FIFTH DAY

The Daily Plan

This week's mandatory behavior:_____

My clearly stated rule:_____

_____

_____

_____

My planned follow-through, if necessary:_____

_____

_____

_____

My planned consistency:_____

_____

_____

_____

The Daily Review

1. Did you clearly state your rule as planned? If not, please review chapters 4 and 7.

2. If it was necessary, did you effectively follow through and enforce the rule as planned? If you didn't, please review chapters 5 and 7.

3. Were you consistent? Did you enforce the rule immediately and until it was obeyed? If not, please review chapters 6 and 7.

4. If you were successful, congratulations. If you were not, review the appropriate sections of the book and start again tomorrow. Don't give up! You will succeed.

The Daily Plan

This week's mandatory behavior:_____

My clearly stated rule:_____

_____

_____

_____

My planned follow-through, if necessary:_____

_____

_____

_____

My planned consistency:_____

_____

_____

_____

The Daily Review

1. Did you clearly state your rule as planned? If not, please review chapters 4 and 7.
2. If it was necessary, did you effectively follow through and enforce the rule as planned? If you didn't, please review chapters 5 and 7.
3. Were you consistent? Did you enforce the rule immediately and until it was obeyed? If not, please review chapters 6 and 7.
4. If you were successful, congratulations. If you were not, review the appropriate sections of the book and start again tomorrow. Don't give up! You will succeed.

FOURTH WEEK—SEVENTH DAY

The Daily Plan

This week's mandatory behavior:_____

My clearly stated rule:_____

_____

_____

_____

My planned follow-through, if necessary:_____

_____

_____

_____

My planned consistency:_____

_____

_____

_____

The Daily Review

1. Did you clearly state your rule as planned? If not, please review chapters 4 and 7.

2. If it was necessary, did you effectively follow through and enforce the rule as planned? If you didn't, please review chapters 5 and 7.

3. Were you consistent? Did you enforce the rule immediately and until it was obeyed? If not, please review chapters 6 and 7.

4. If you were successful, congratulations. If you were not, review the appropriate sections of the book and start again tomorrow. Don't give up! You will succeed.

Index